Port Elgin Ontario Book 2 and Area in Colour Photos, Saving Our History One Photo at a Time

Photography
by Barbara Raué
2014

Series Name:
Cruising Ontario

Book 108: Port Elgin Book 2

Cover photo: 697 Gustavus Street, see Page 37

Series Name: Cruising Ontario
Saving Our History One Photo at a Time
in colour photos

Book 33: Southampton
Book 34: Jarvis
Book 35: Hagersville
Book 36: Caledonia
Book 37: Simcoe
Book 38-41: Cambridge
Book 42-43: Kitchener
Book 46: Shelburne
Book 47: Alton, Mono
Book 48: London Colour
Book 49: St. Thomas
Book 50-52: Orangeville
Book 53-55: Dundas
Book 56: Stratford
Book 57: Hanover
Book 58-59: New Hamburg
Book 60: Waterdown
Book 61: Burlington
Book 62: Stoney Creek
Book 63: Seaforth
Book 64: Aberfoyle, Morriston and Rockton
Book 65: Eden Mills
Book 66: Ancaster and Mount Hope
Book 67: Jarvis,Pt.Dover
Book 68-69: Fergus, Elora
Book 70-71: Elmira
Book72:St.Jacobs, St.Clements, Heidelberg,Crosshill,Bamberg

Book 73: Linwood, Macton
Book 74: Wellesley
Book 75: Listowel
Book 76: Palmerston
Book 77:Dorchester to Aylmer
Book 78-79: Aylmer
Book 80: Drayton & Area
Book 81: Tillsonburg
Book 82: Arthur
Book 83: Rockwood
Book 84: Acton
Book 85-86: Guelph
Book 87-91: Hamilton
Book 92-93: Owen Sound
Book 94: Oakville
Book 95: Brantford
Book 96: Mount Forest
Book 97: Orillia
Book 98: Ayr
Book 99-101: Peterborough
Book 102-104: Niagara on Lake
Book 105: Harrison,Clifford
Book 106: Neustadt
Book 107-108: Port Elgin
Book 109: Wingham

Other Books by Barbara Raue

Coins of Gold

Arrows, Indians and Love

The Life and Times of Barbara
Volume 1: Inventions That Have Enhanced My Life
Volume 2: Entertainment That I Have Enjoyed
Volume 3: East Coast Trips
Volume 4: Olympics Have Always Intrigued Me
Volume 5: Wonders of the World
Volume 6: Caribbean Cruises We Have Enjoyed
Volume 7: Animals
Volume 8: Storms and Other Major Disasters in My Lifetime
Volume 9: Wars, Terrorist Attacks and Major Disasters

The Cromwell Family Book

Laura Secord Discovered

Daddy Where Are You?

Visit Barbara's website to view all of her books
http://barbararaue.ca

Port Elgin

In 1854, Benjamin Shantz acquired a sawmill on Mill Creek from George Butchart. Nearby he built a gristmill and within three years a community of 250 people developed around these mills. Stores, hotels and tanneries were built and a village plot for Port Elgin was laid out in 1857. Businessmen Henry Hilker, Samuel Bricker, and John Stafford contributed to the development of the settlement. The original economic development of Port Elgin during the 19th century was based on its harbour facilities on Lake Huron constructed in 1857–1858 making the village a distribution centre for the surrounding agricultural region. The arrival of the Wellington, Grey and Bruce Railway in 1872 further stimulated the growth of the community.

Chatsworth

Chatsworth is located on the Toronto-Sydenham Road, Highway 10, south of Owen Sound (formerly called Sydenham).

The northern terminus of the early colonization road, The Toronto-Sydenham Road, was located near here at its junction with the Garafraxa Road. Free grants of fifty acre lots were given to persons fulfilling the settlement duties, and by 1851 about four hundred families had moved here.

Dornoch

The village of Dornoch is located about 11 kilometers north of the Town of Durham on Highway 6 in Grey County. It is part of Chatsworth Township. Dornoch is 11 kilometers south of Williamsford and 33 kilometers south of Owen Sound.

Dornoch was settled by Bartholomew Griffin in 1841. The area was originally called "Griffin's Corners". Griffin started the first general store. The village is primarily a small farming community, but has a convenience store that is known for its photography and ice cream, a community hall, as well as the recently rebuilt Dawg House Inn.

Table of Contents

Port Elgin

Market Street		Page 6
Goderich Street		Page 13
George Street		Page 14
Hilker Street		Page 23
Mill Street		Page 24
Catherine Street		Page 31
Bricker Street		Page 34
Gustavus Street		Page 33

Chatsworth   Page 38

Dornoch   Page 44

Architectural Terms   Page 46

Building Styles   Page 49

Port Elgin

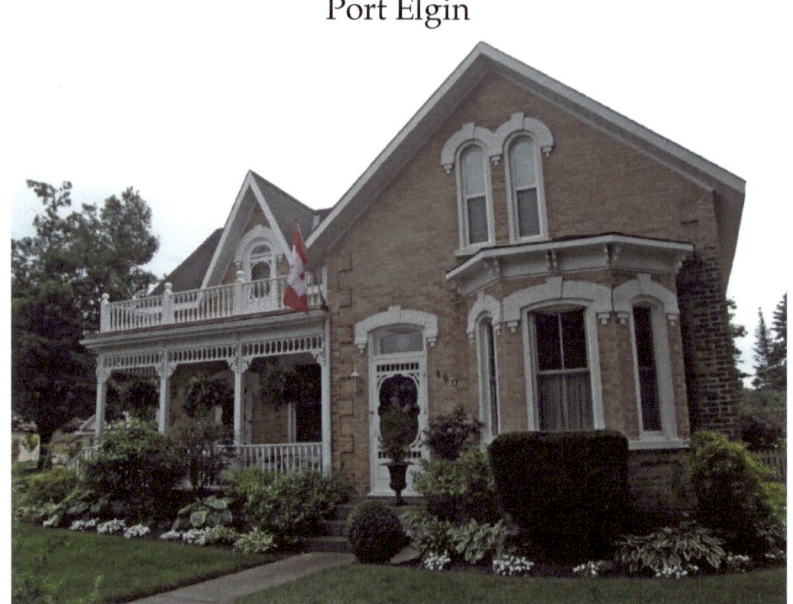

480 Market Street – yellow brick – Gothic Revival, arched voussoirs and keystones, bay window with cornice brackets

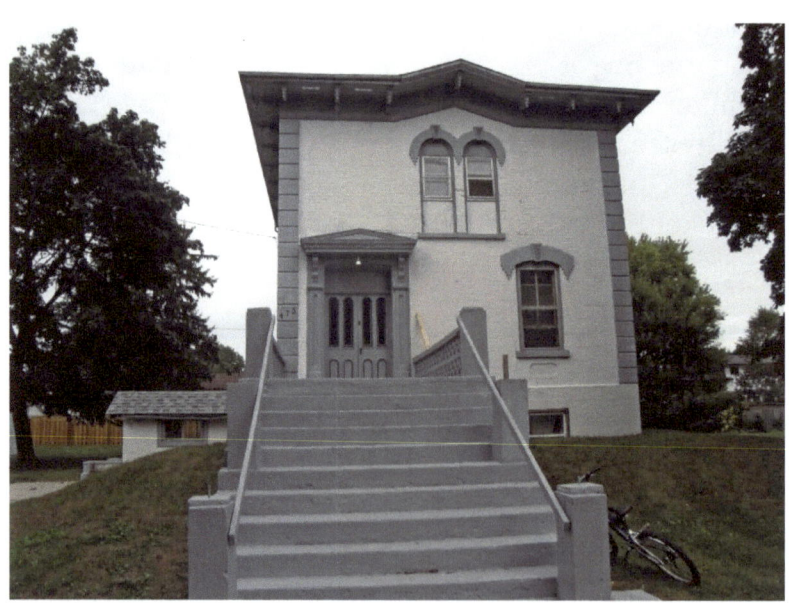

473 Market Street - Italianate style, arched voussoirs and keystones

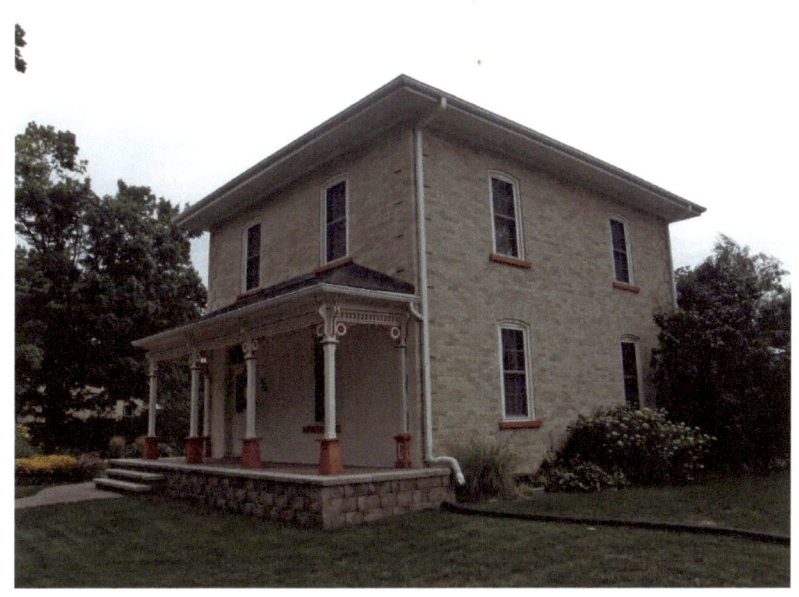

490 Market Street – yellow brick, Italianate style,
corner quoins

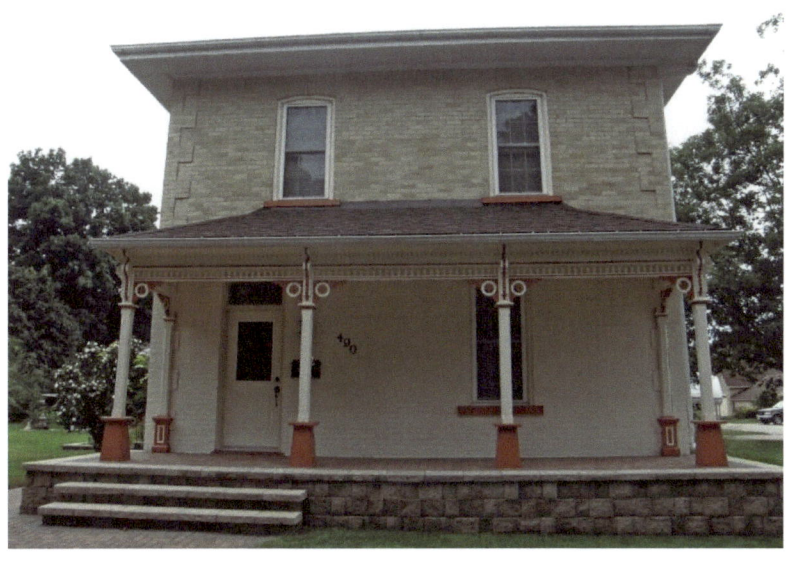

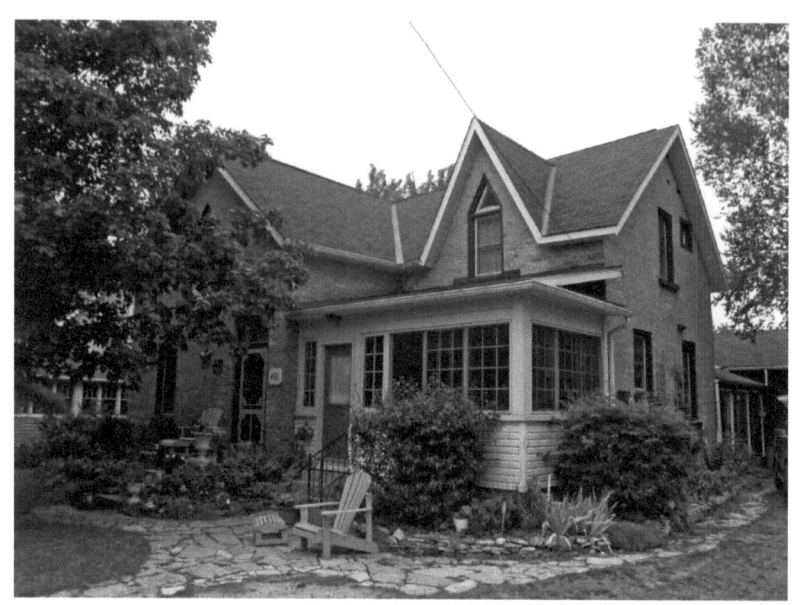

Gothic Revival

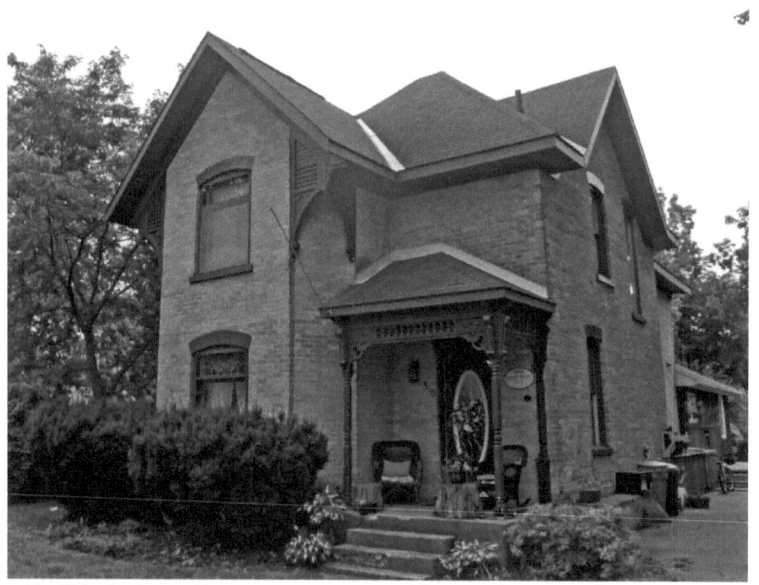

518 Market Street – Ernest Vaupel, Builder – 1890
Yellow brick - large fretwork pieces resembling brackets

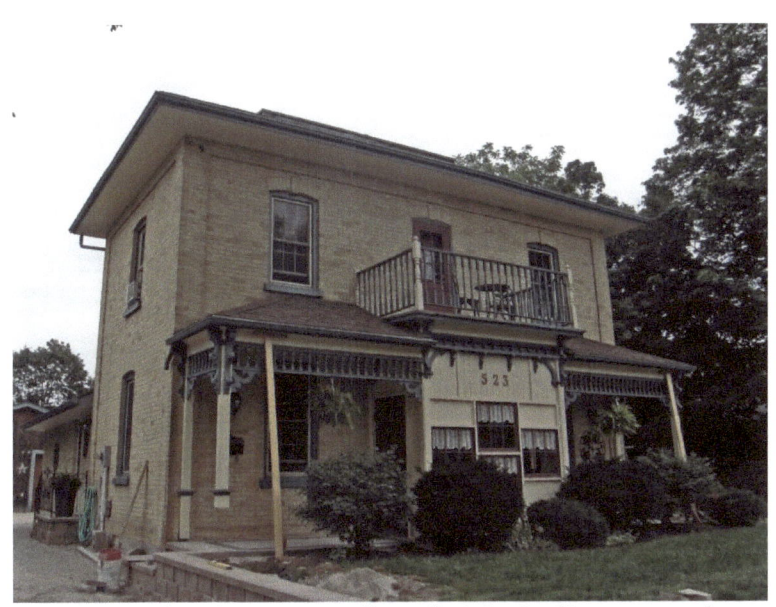

523 Market Street – yellow brick, Italianate style, 2nd floor balcony

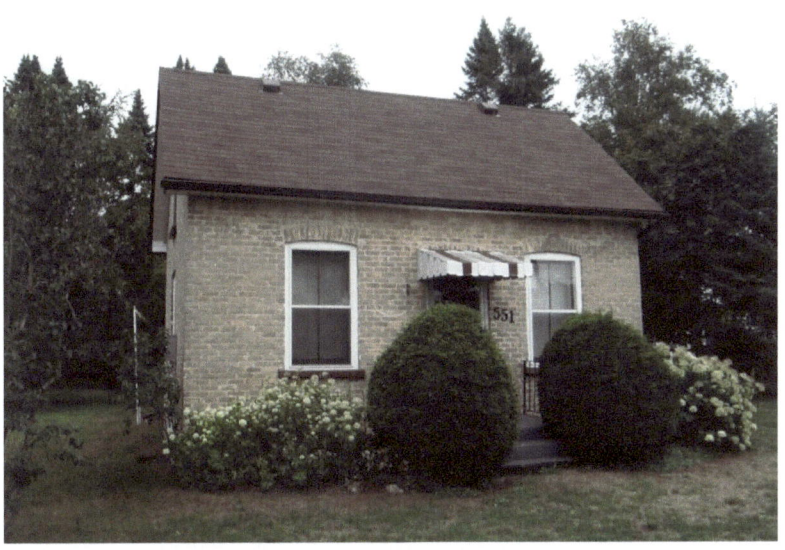

551 Market Street – Gothic Revival 1½ storey

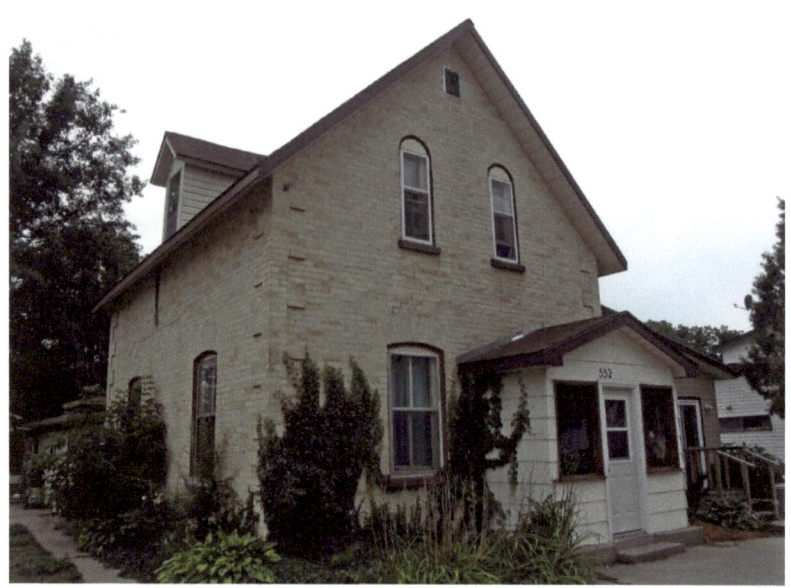

552 Market Street – yellow brick, Gothic Revival style,
Corner quoins

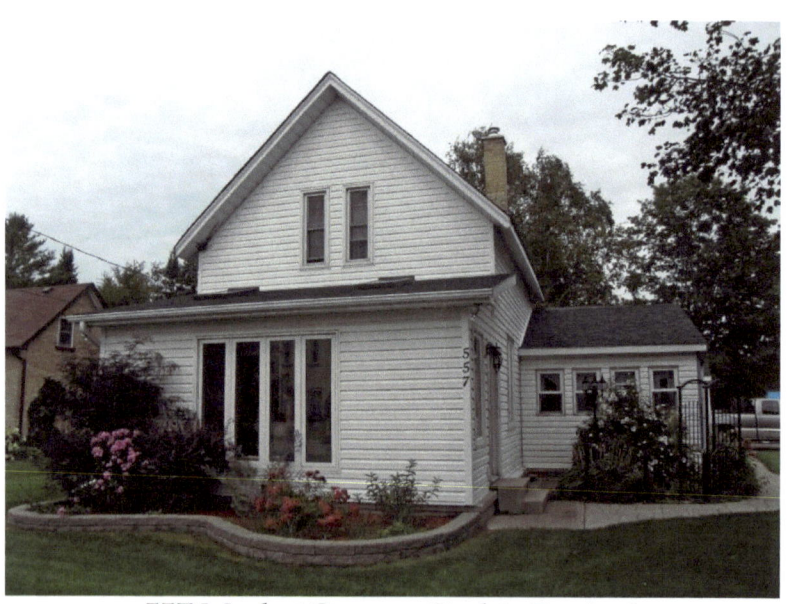

557 Market Street – Gothic Revival
– upgraded with white siding

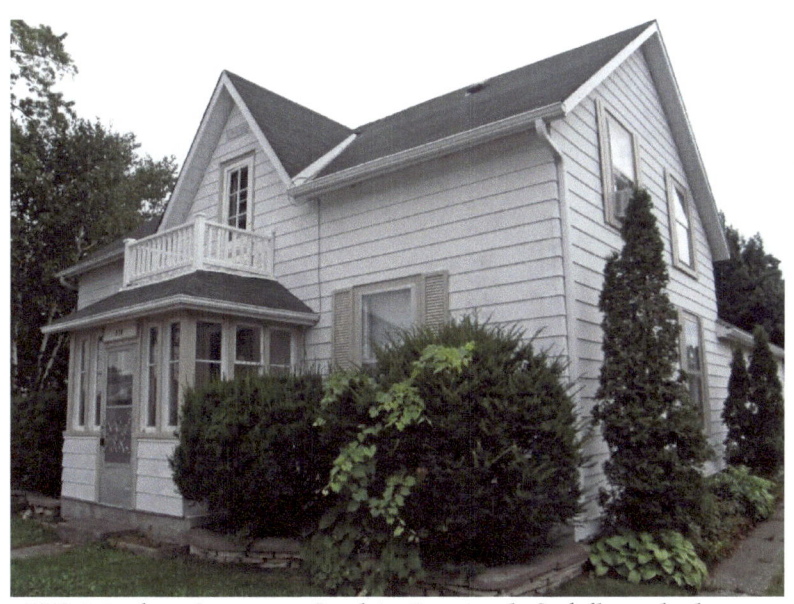

578 Market Street – Gothic Revival, 2nd floor balcony

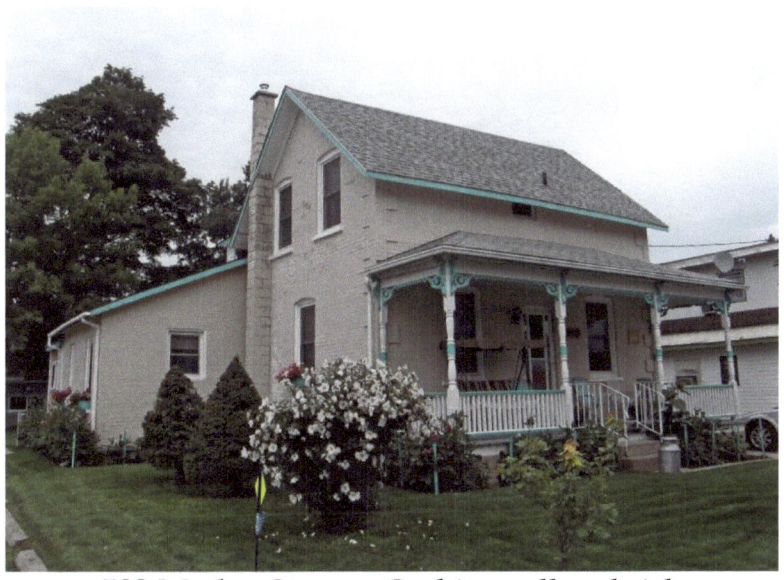

583 Market Street – Gothic - yellow brick

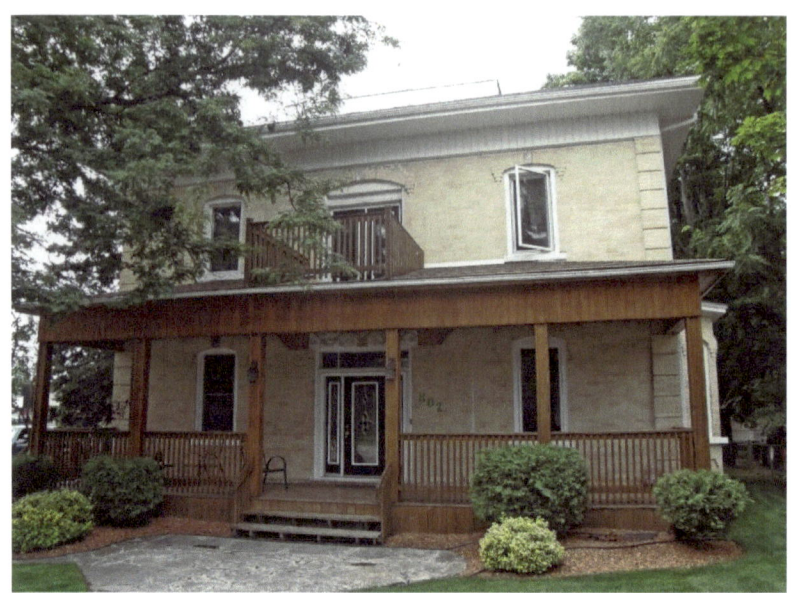

802 Market Street – Italianate style – hipped roof, yellow brick, corner quoins

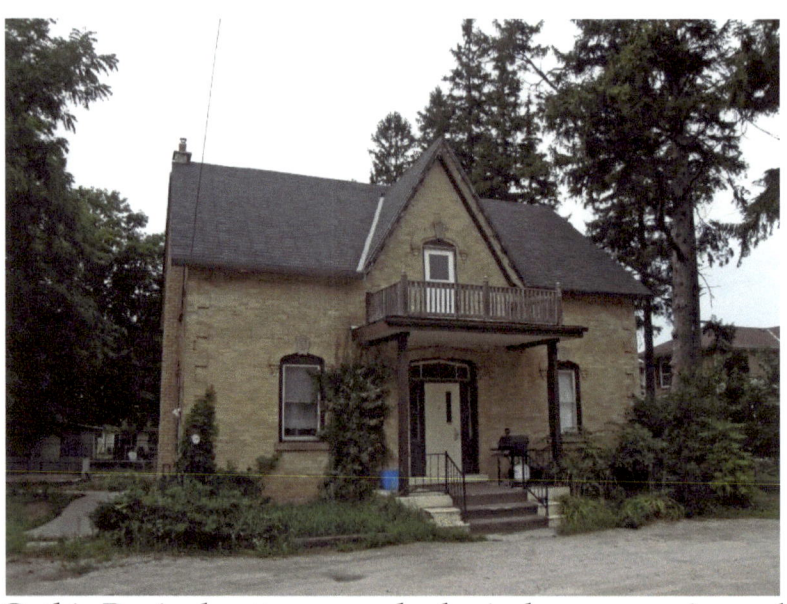

Gothic Revival cottage – arched window voussoirs and keystones, corner quoins, 2nd floor balcony

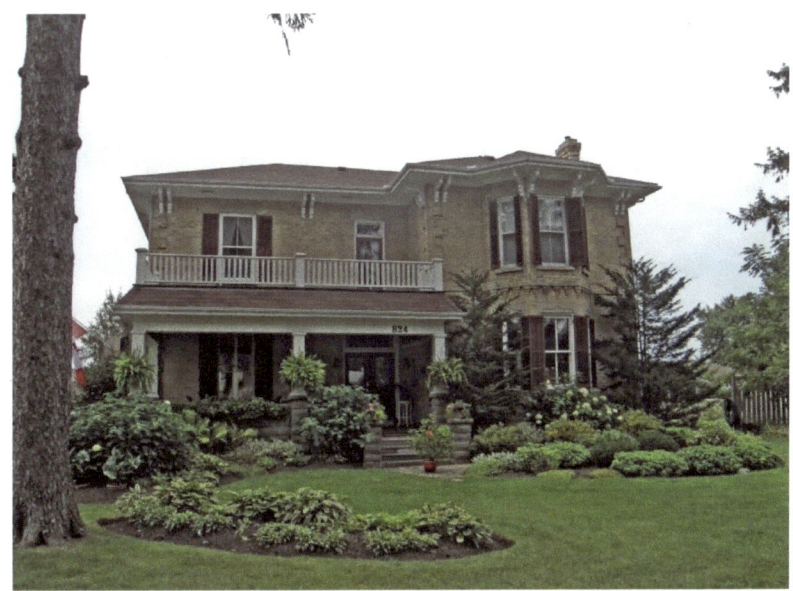

824 Goderich Street – Sprucehall Bed and Breakfast
Italianate style, paired cornice brackets,
Two storey bay window, 2nd floor balcony

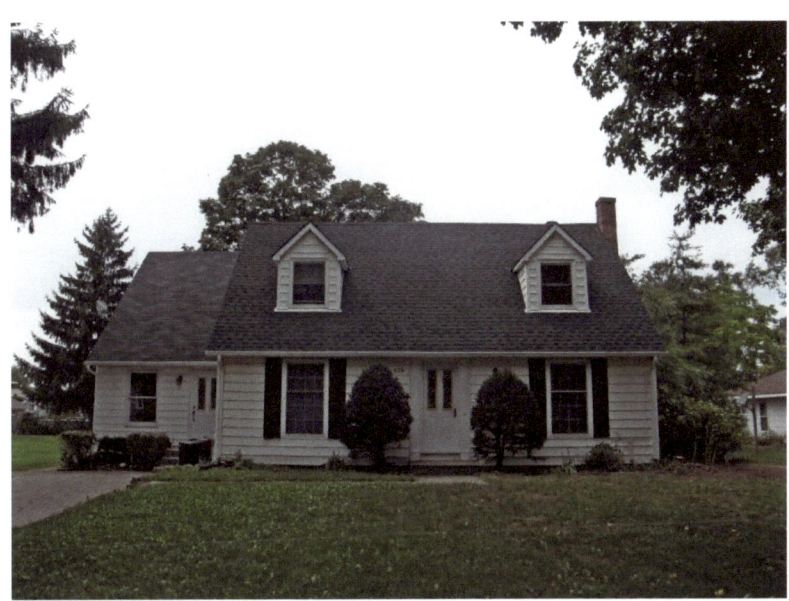

850 Goderich Street – Gothic Revival cottage,dormers in attic

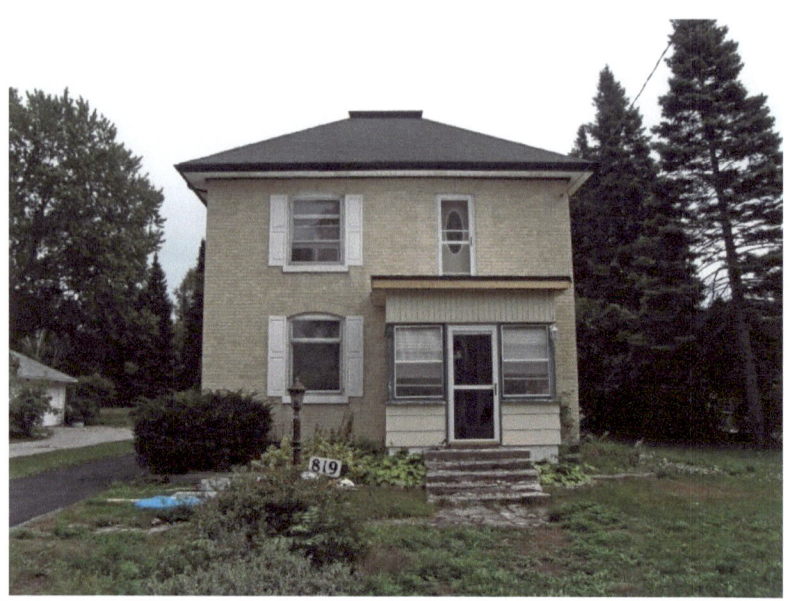

819 George Street – yellow brick, Italianate style, hipped roof

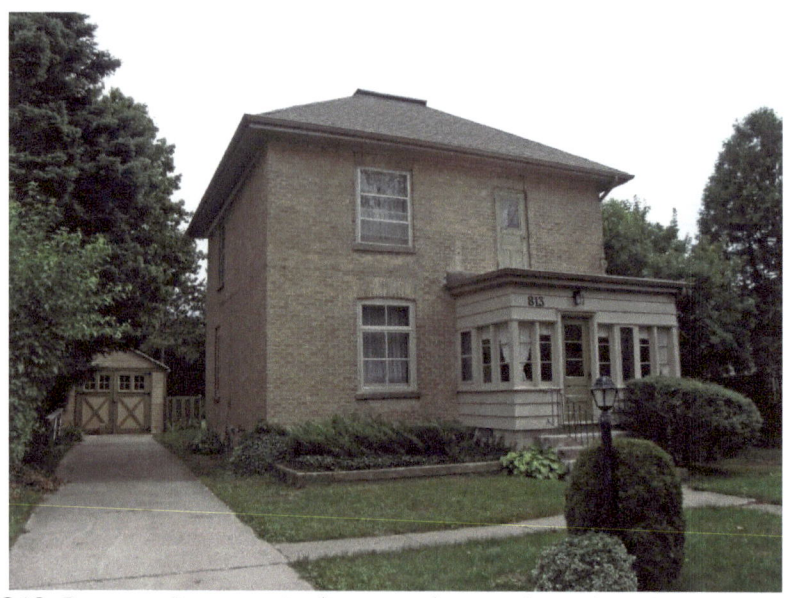

813 George Street – Italianate, hipped roof, yellow brick

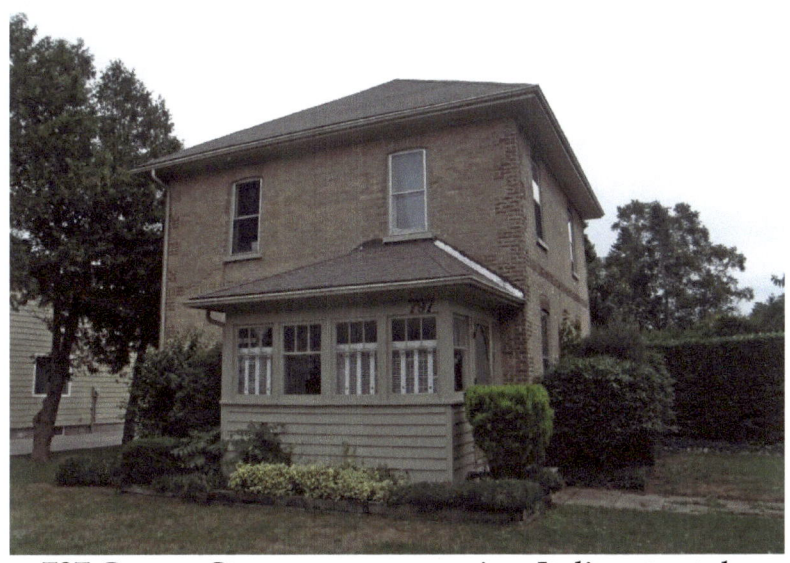

797 George Street – corner quoins, Italianate style, Hipped roof

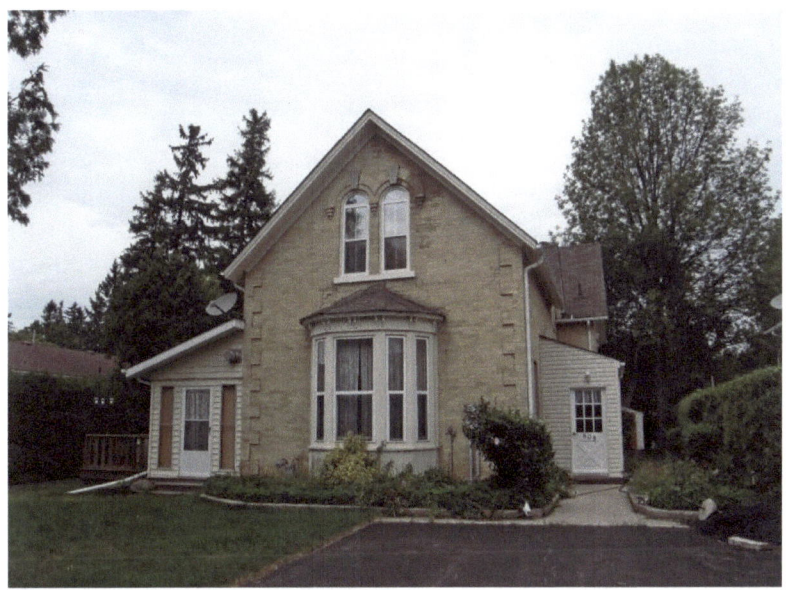

609 George Street – Gothic Revival, arched voussoirs and keystones, bay window with cornice brackets, corner quoins

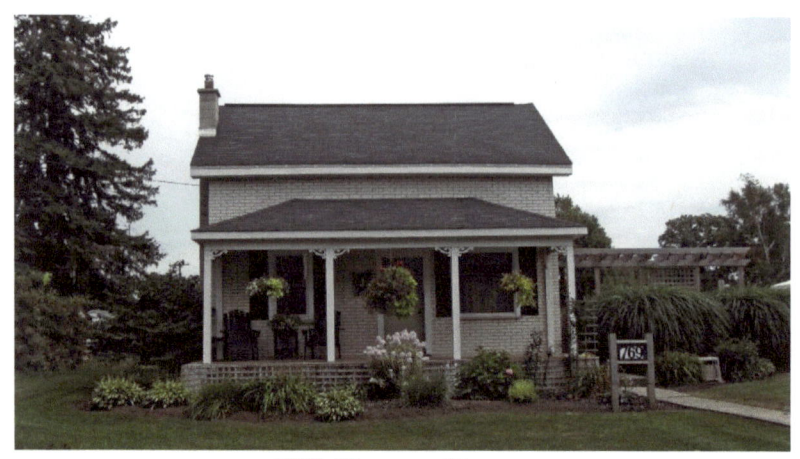

769 George Street

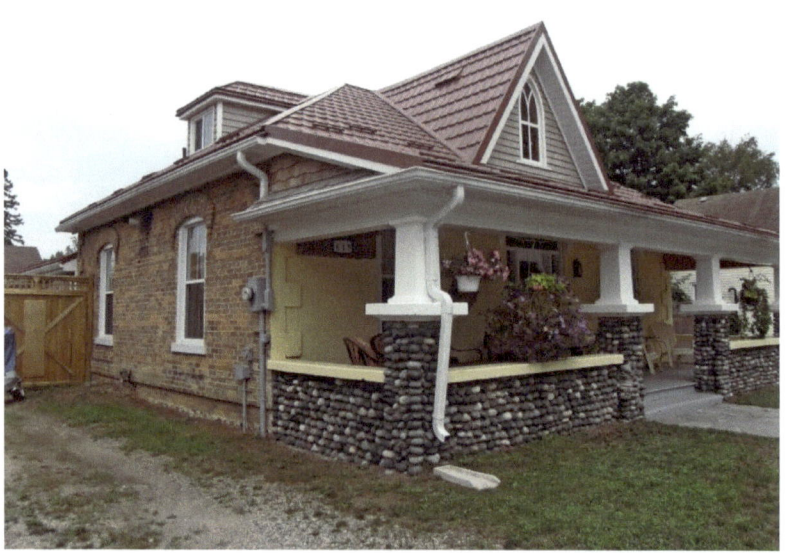

649 Market Street – yellow brick, cottage with dormer on side, and arched gable above verandah

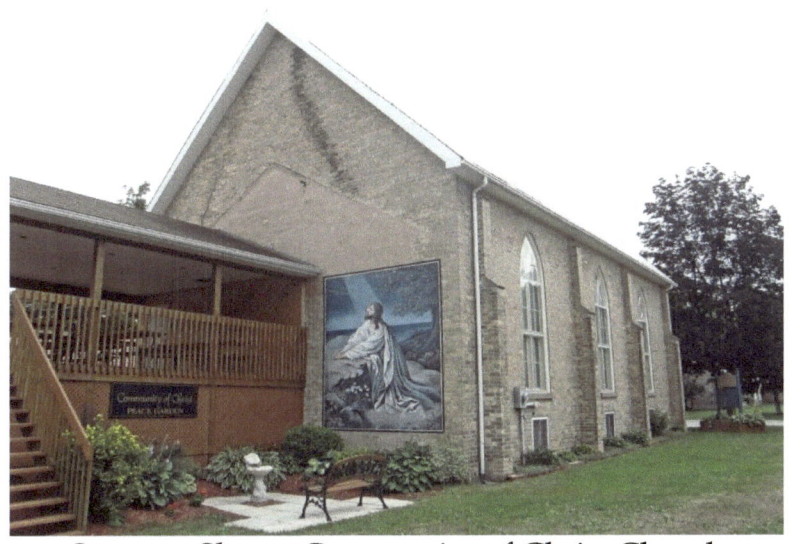

Saugeen Shores Community of Christ Church
641 Market Street at corner of Bricker – Gothic Revival

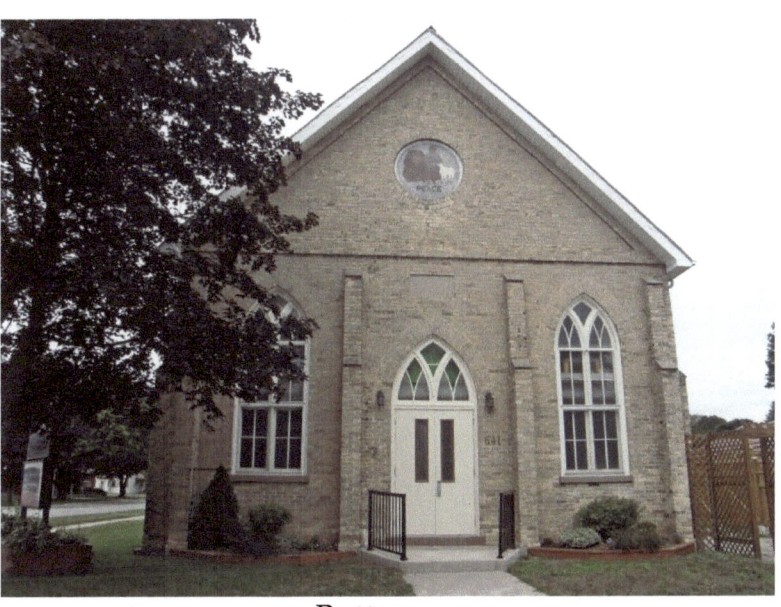

Buttresses

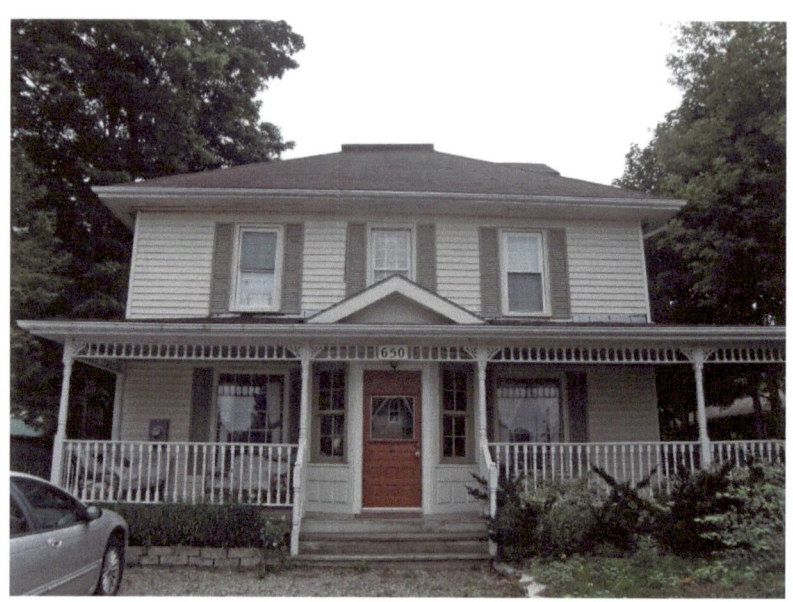

650 Market Street - Georgian style

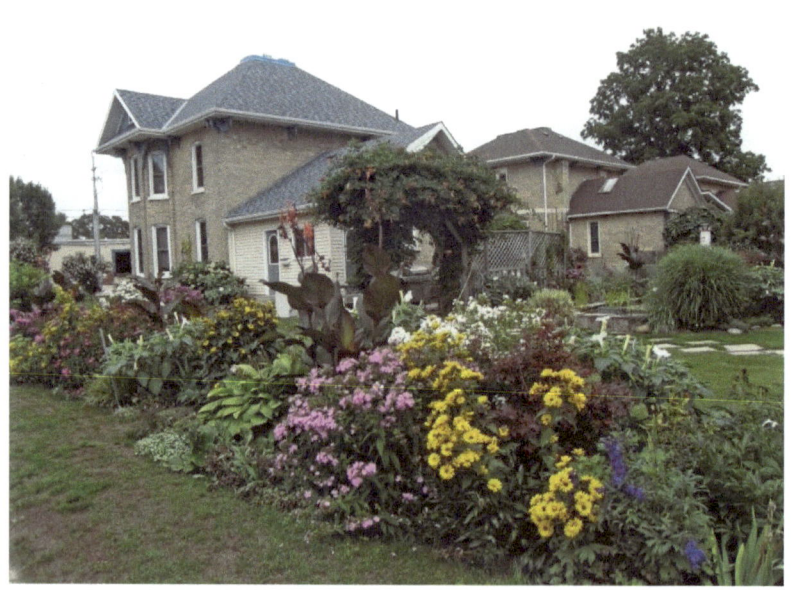

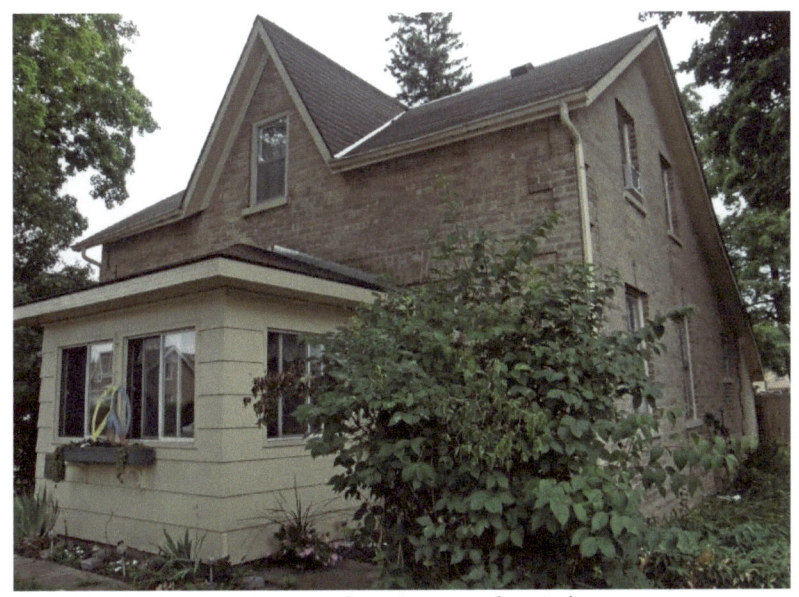

656 Market Street – Gothic Revival – 1½ storeys, corner quoins, yellow brick

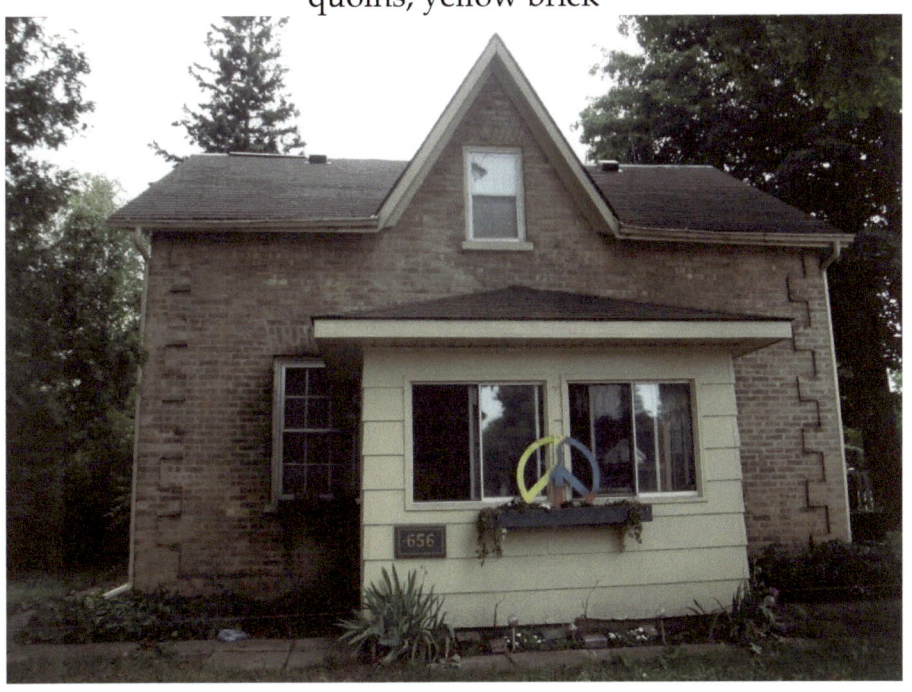

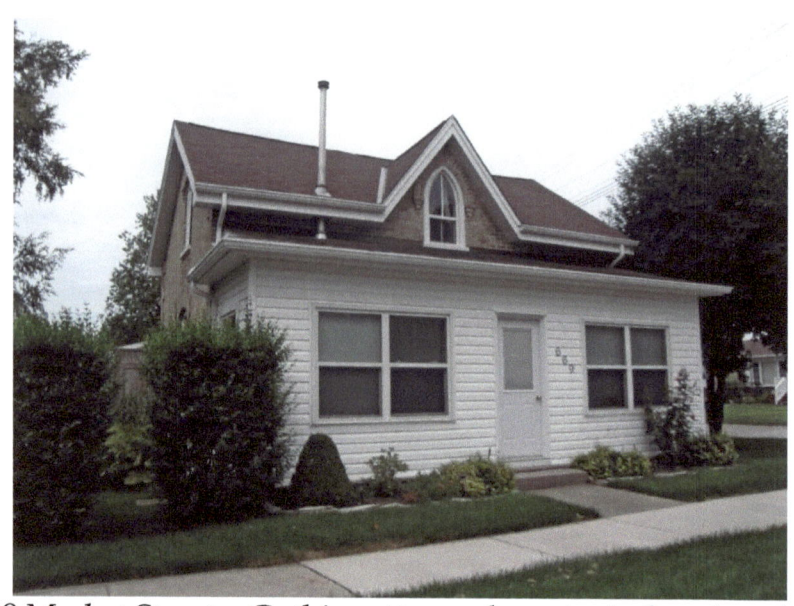

669 Market Street – Gothic cottage – lancet window in gable, original yellow brick

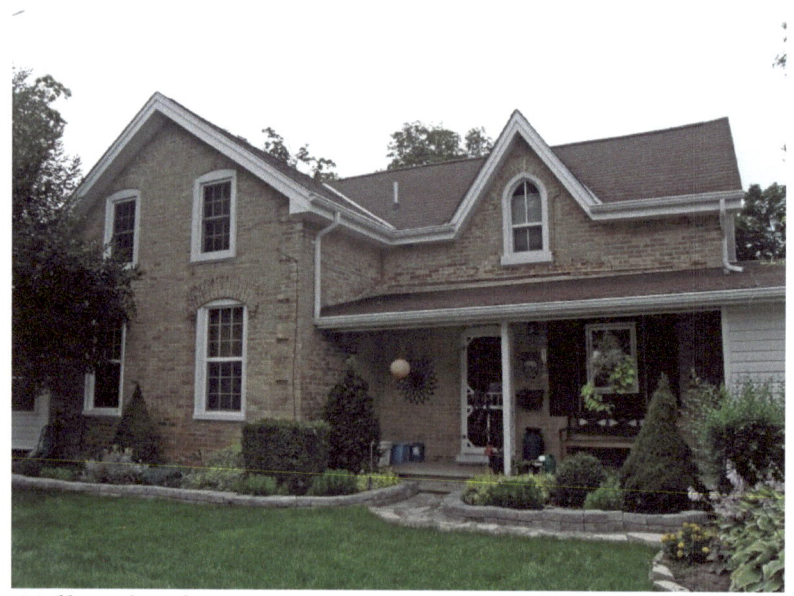

Yellow brick – Gothic Revival style, arched voussoirs

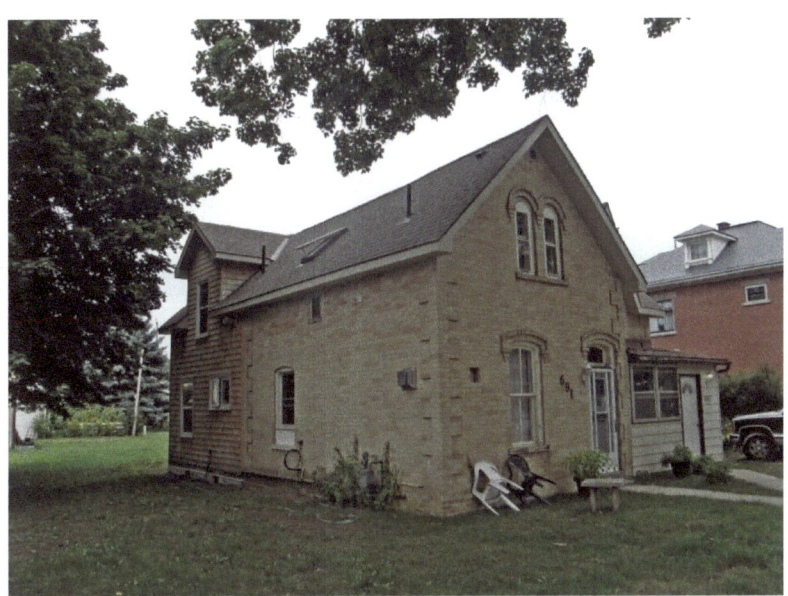

691 Market Street – yellow brick, Gothic Revival, 1½ storey, decorative voussoirs, corner quoins

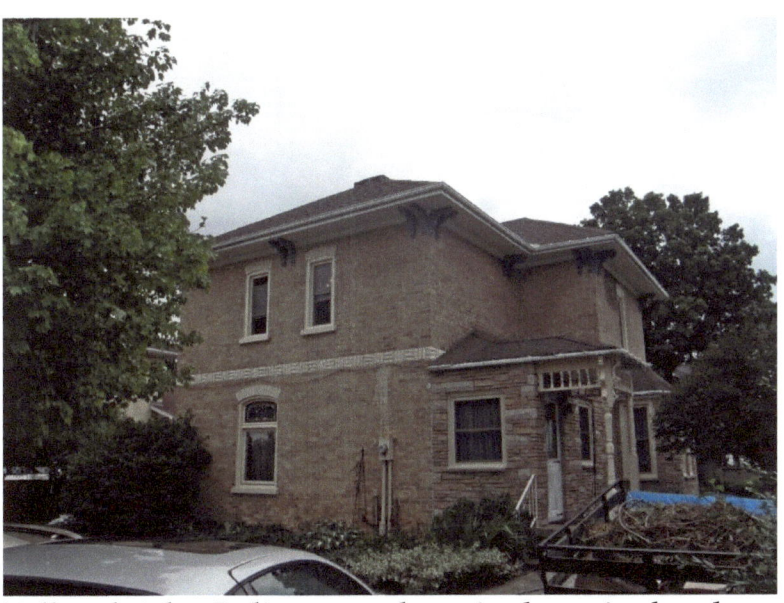

Yellow brick – Italianate style, paired cornice brackets, dichromatic banding, buff coloured voussoirs

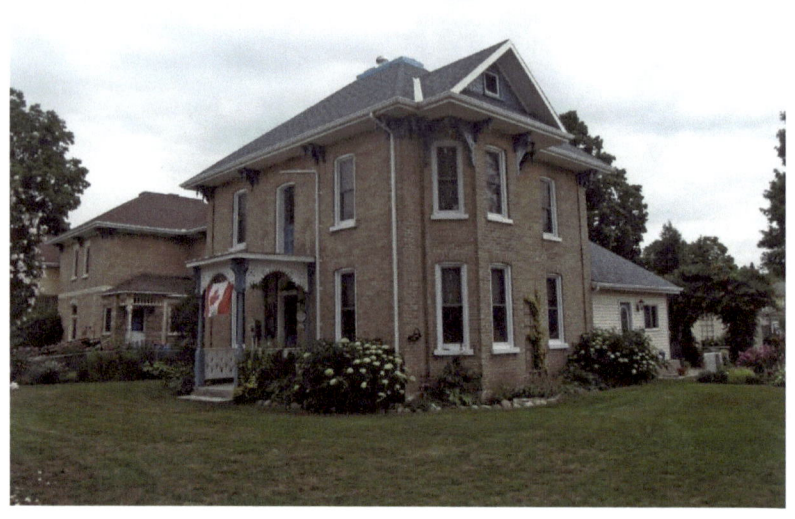

684 Market Street – John C. Kennedy, Grain Dealer – circa 1877 – yellow brick, Italianate style, paired cornice brackets

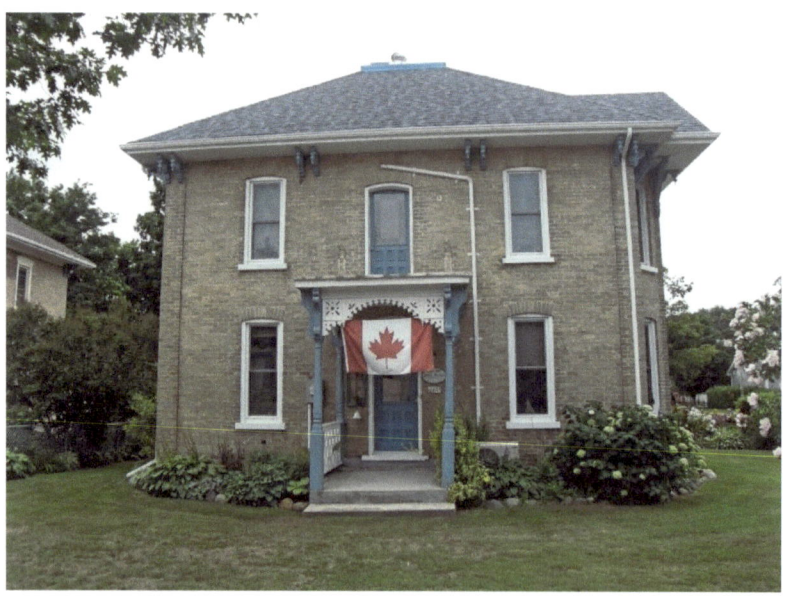

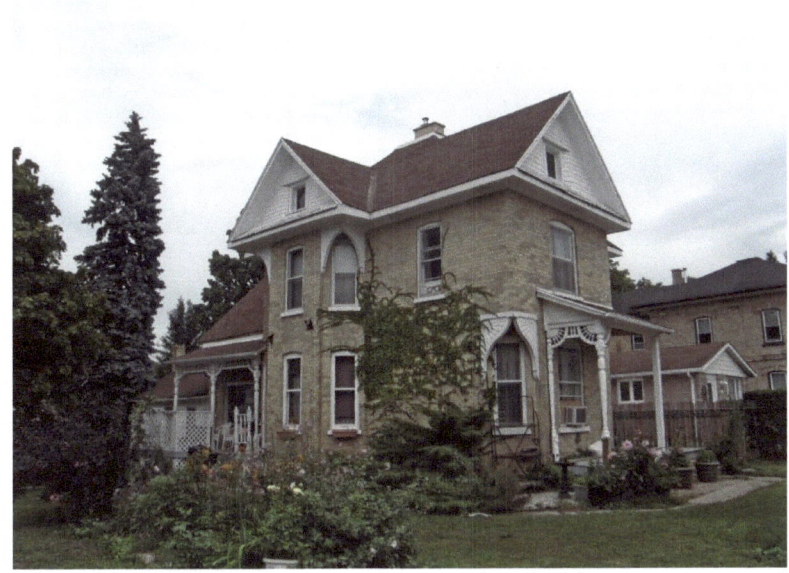

Yellow brick – Edwardian - two-and-a-half storey tower-like
bay with projecting eaves and large fretwork pieces
resembling brackets – matching fretwork piece over lower
window to left of porch and below porch roof

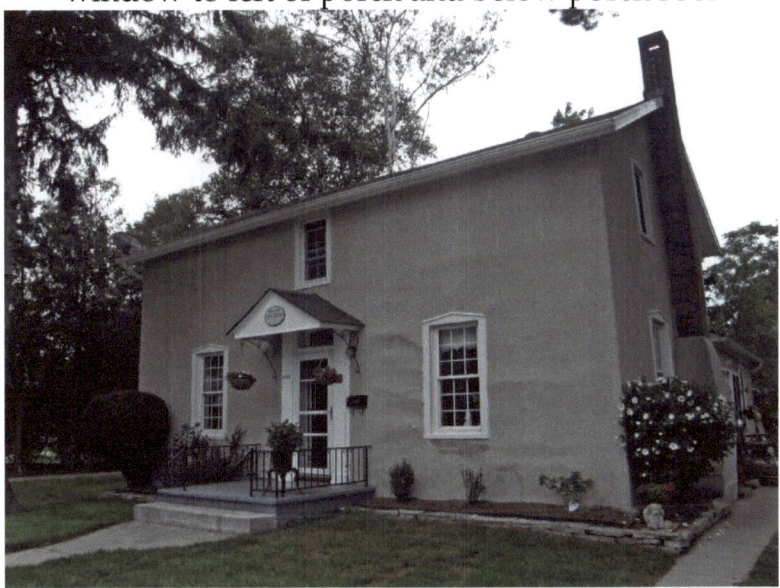

660 Hilker Street – Samuel Roether, Gaoler – c. 1870 – stucco

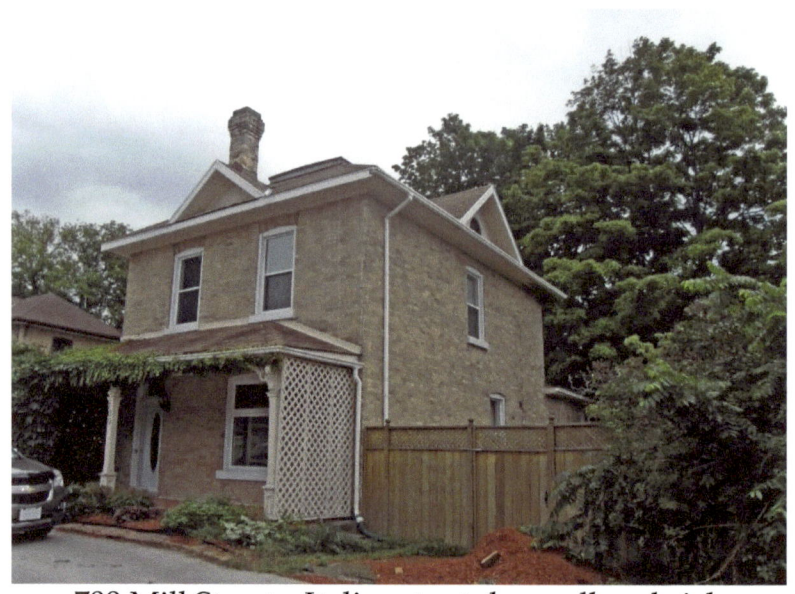

700 Mill Street - Italianate style – yellow brick

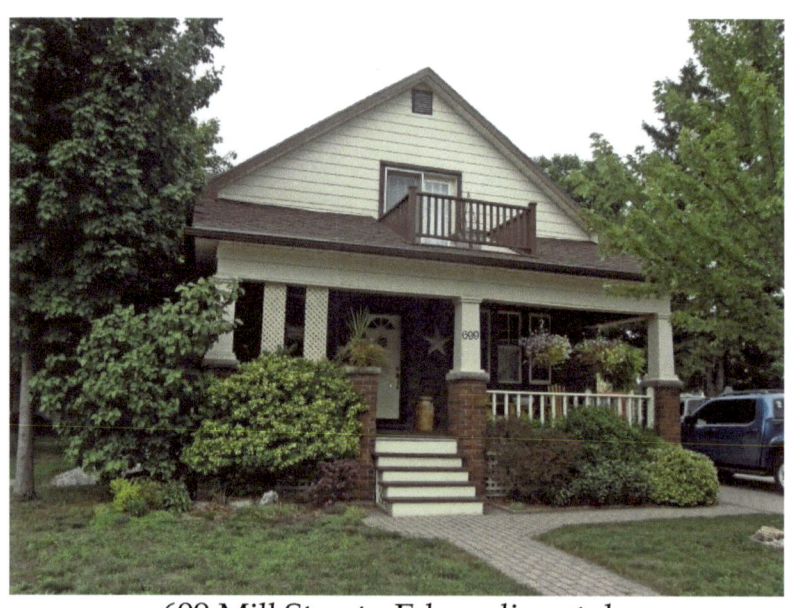

699 Mill Street - Edwardian style

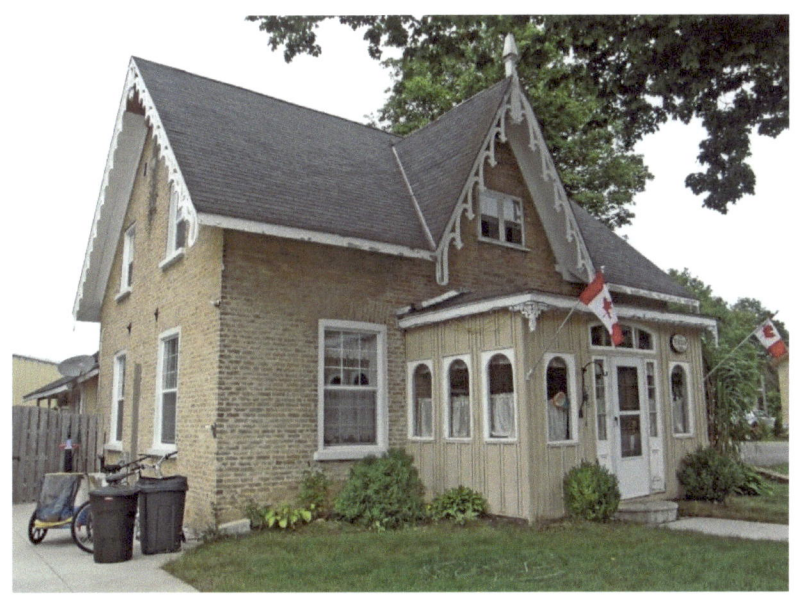

709 Mill Street – Gothic Revival – Vergeboard trim on gables – yellow brick

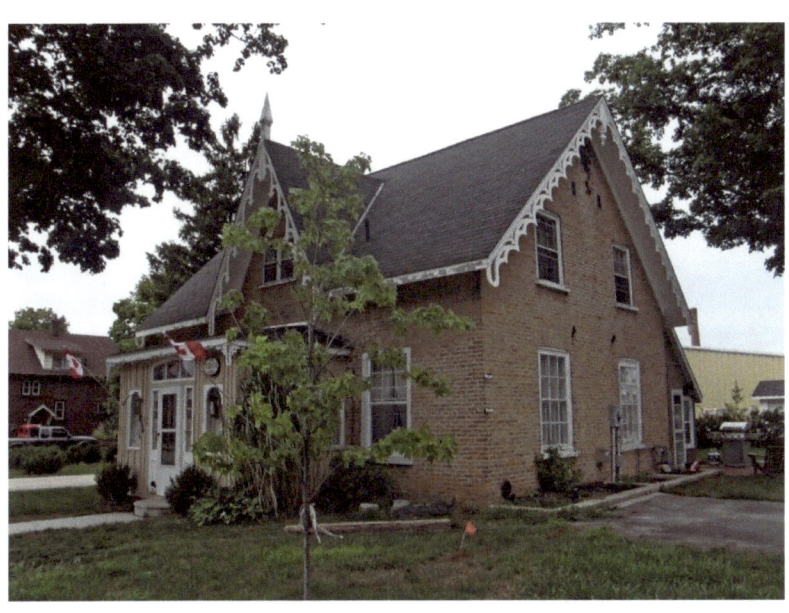

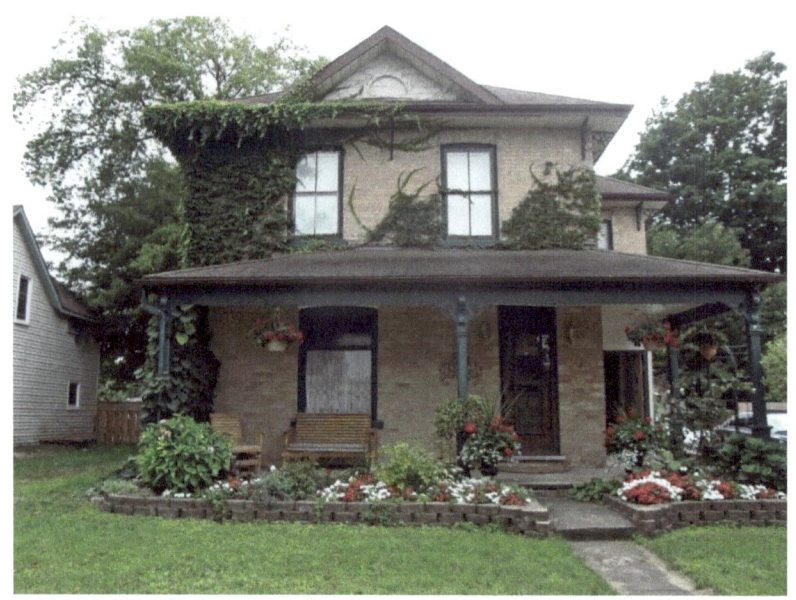

706 Mill Street – Italianate style – yellow brick

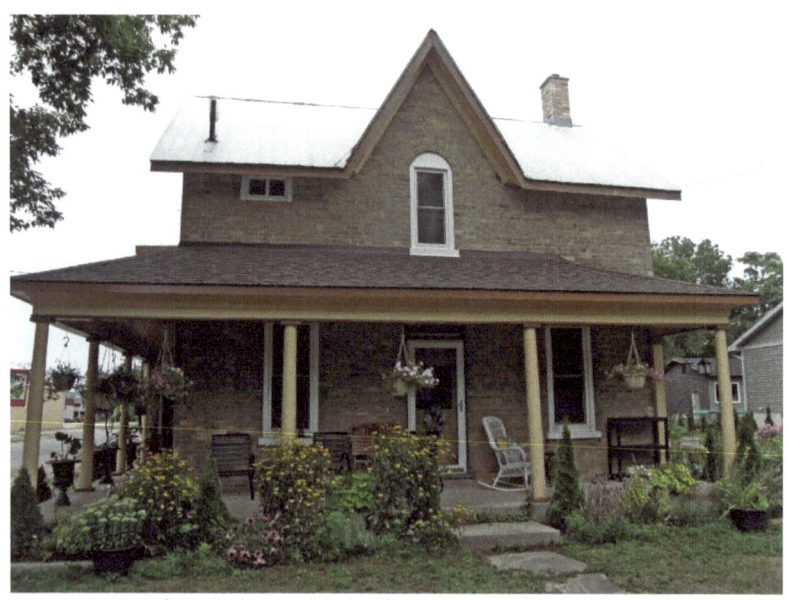

Gothic Revival – 1½ storey, yellow brick

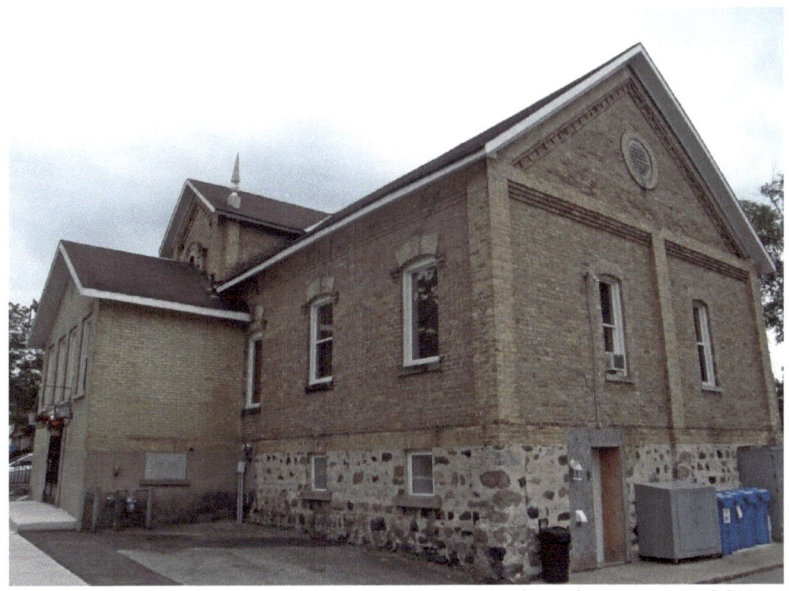

742 Mill Street - Port Elgin High School – A.D. 1925 -
Cobblestone basement, Yellow brick, dentil moulding on
gable end, arched voussoirs

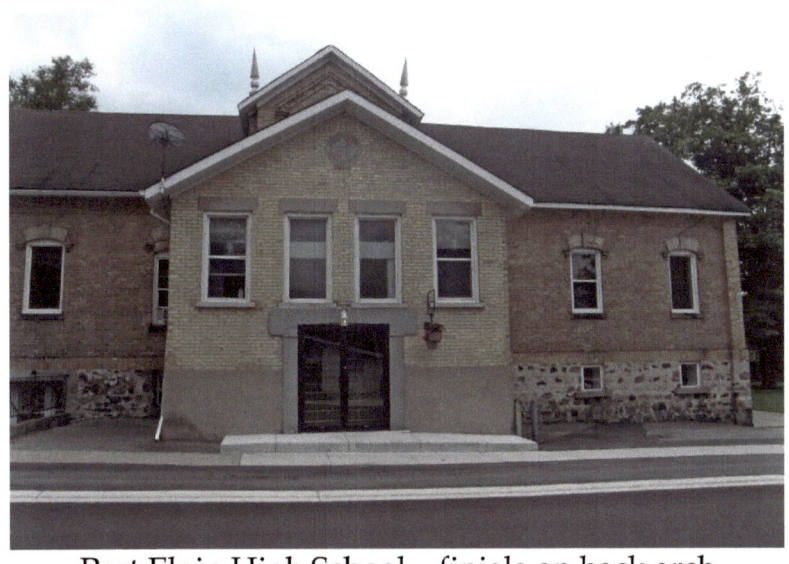

Port Elgin High School – finials on back arch

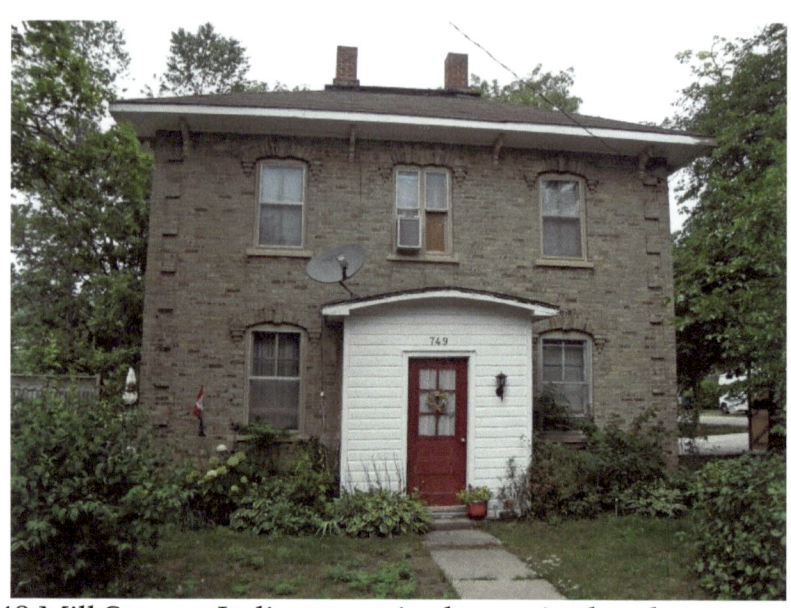

749 Mill Street – Italianate – single cornice brackets, corner quoins, decorative voussoirs

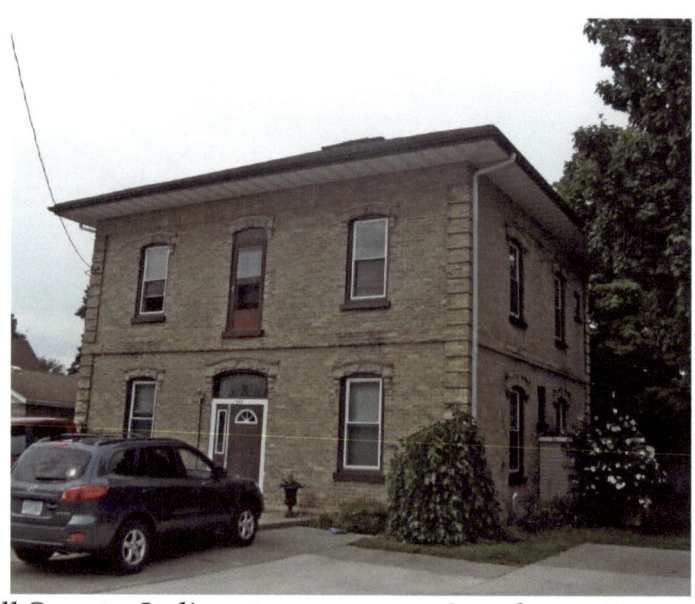

695 Mill Street – Italianate, corner quoins, decorative voussoirs

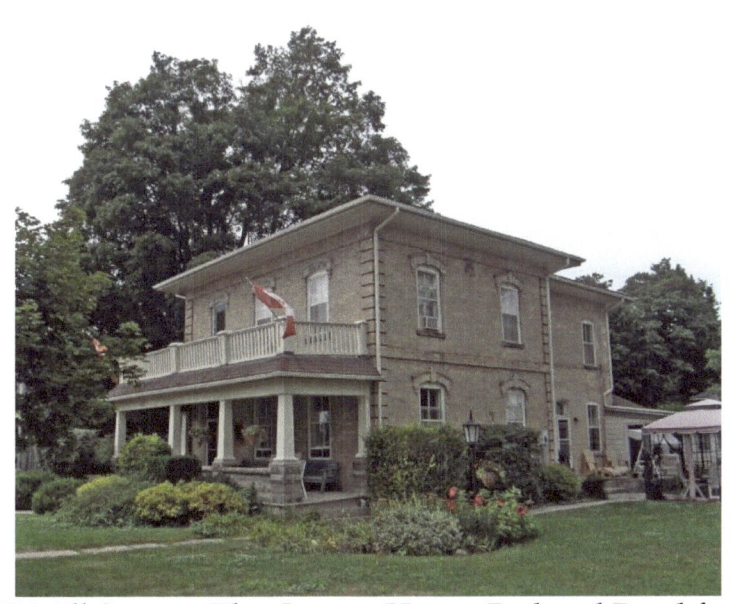

657 Mill Street – The George House Bed and Breakfast - Italianate style

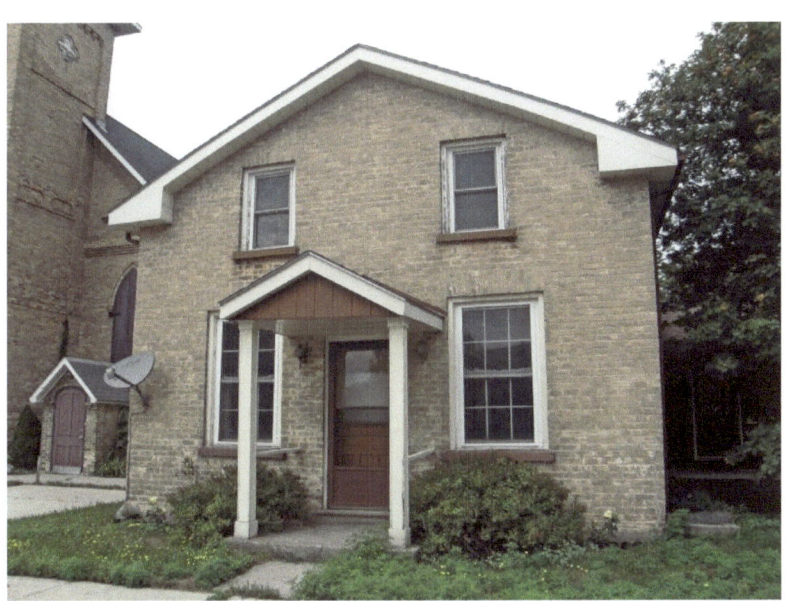

Gothic Revival, yellow brick, cornice return on gable

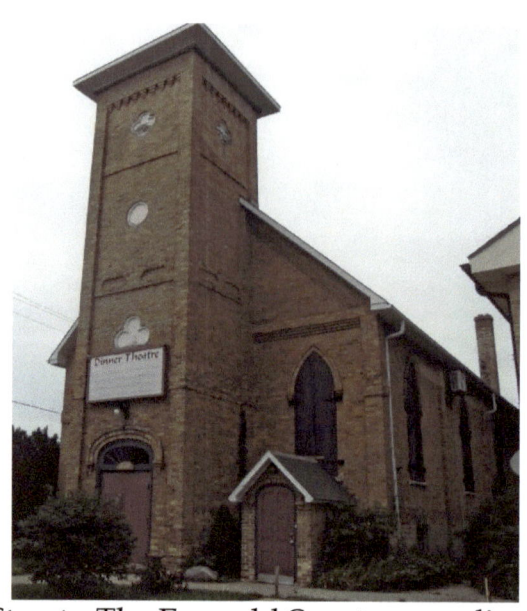

643 Mill Street - The Emerald Sanctuary – dinner theatre
– yellow brick

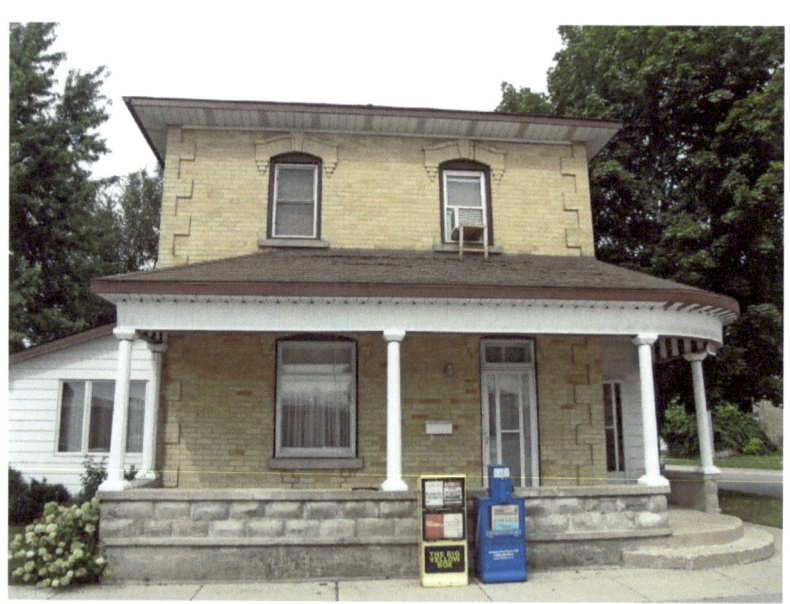

Italianate – yellow brick, decorative voussoirs and keystones,
corner quoining

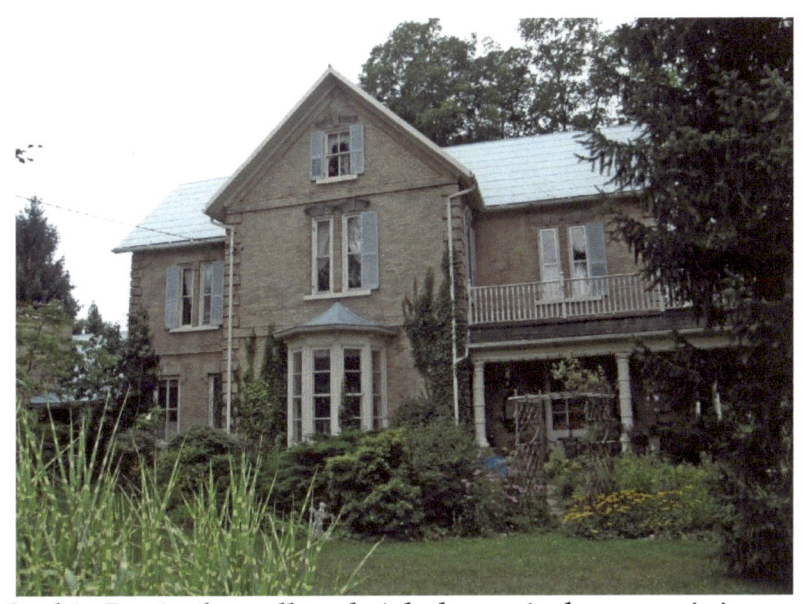

Gothic Revival – yellow brick, bay window, quoining on corners, decorative voussoirs and keystones

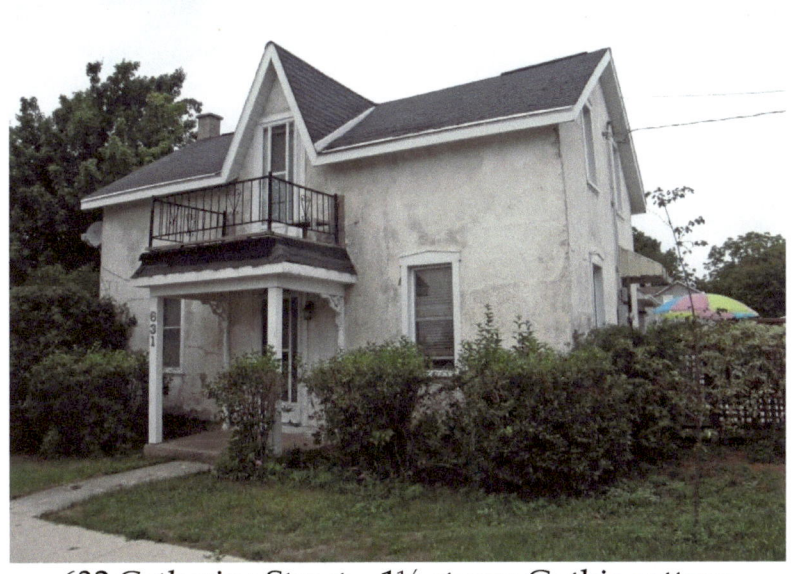

632 Catherine Street – 1½ storey Gothic cottage – plaster exterior

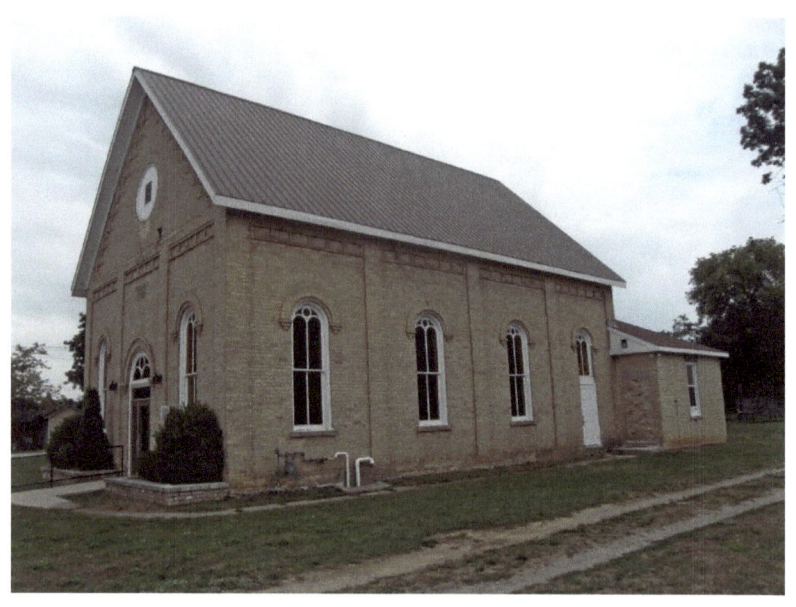

Regular Baptist Church A.D. 1878

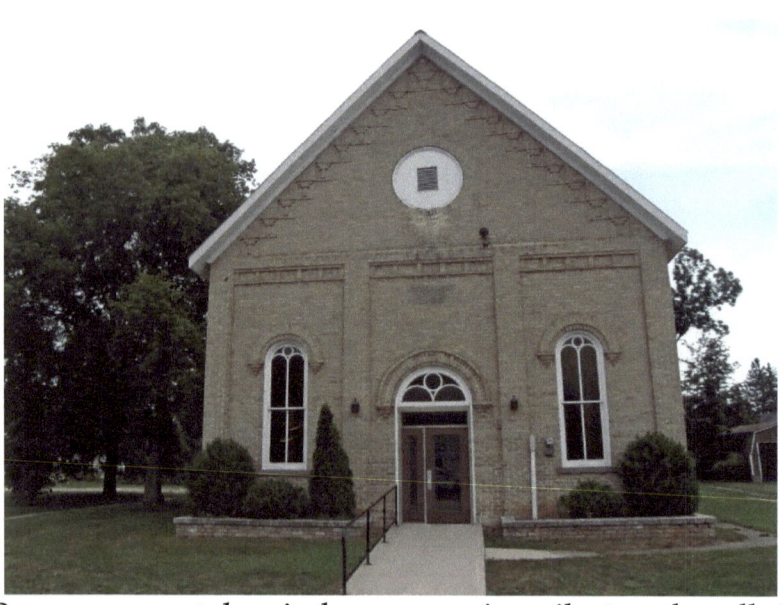

Romanesque style window voussoirs, pilasters, bevelled
dentil moulding

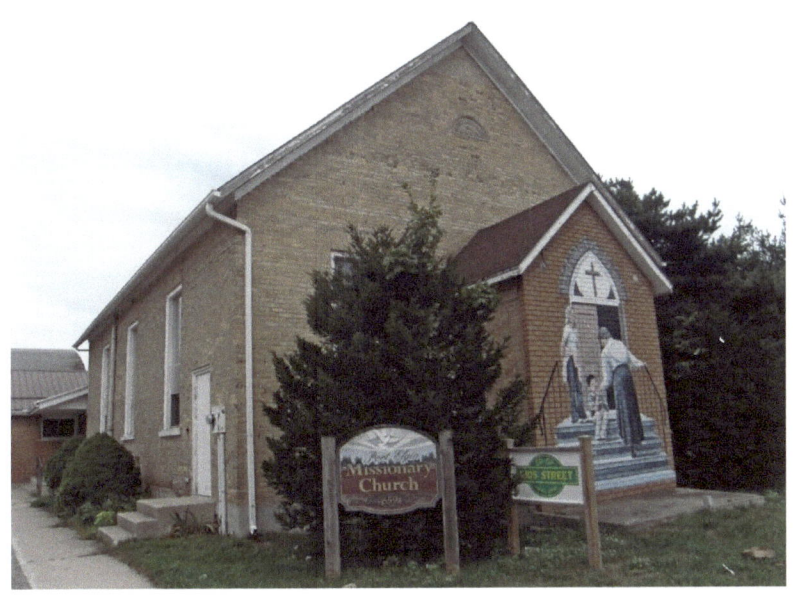

659 Gustavus Street - Port Elgin Missionary Church
(United Mennonite Church A.D. 1875)

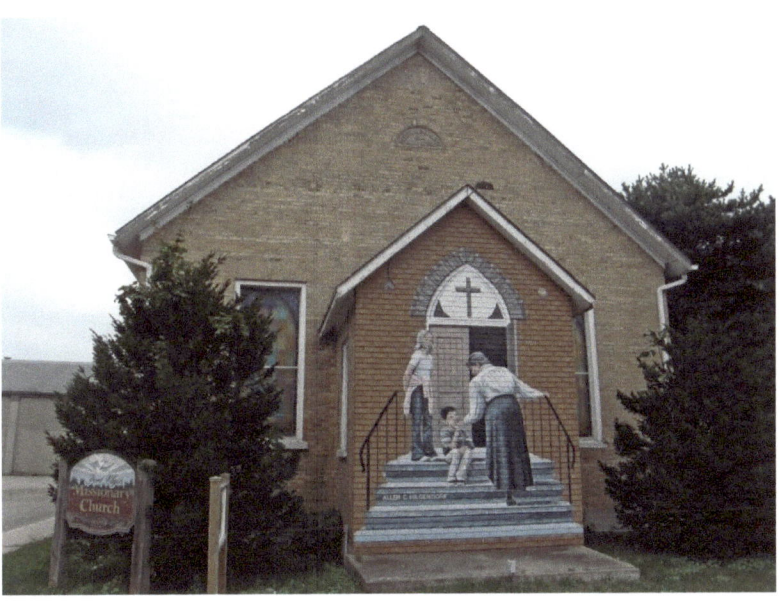

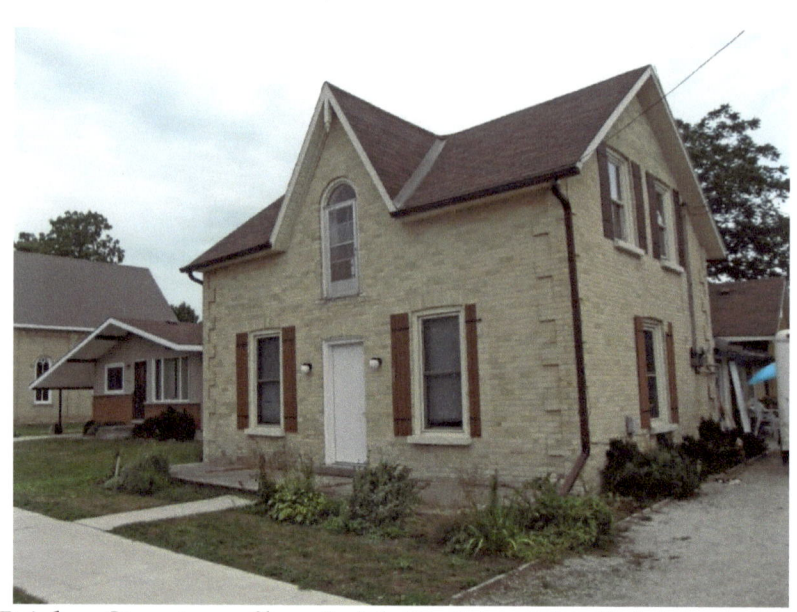

Bricker Street – yellow brick Gothic style, finial on gable. Corner quoins

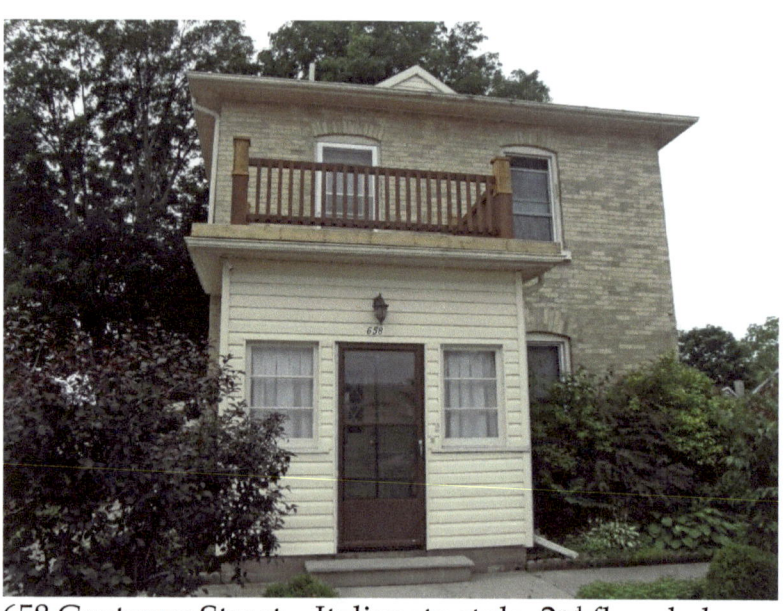

658 Gustavus Street – Italianate style, 2nd floor balcony

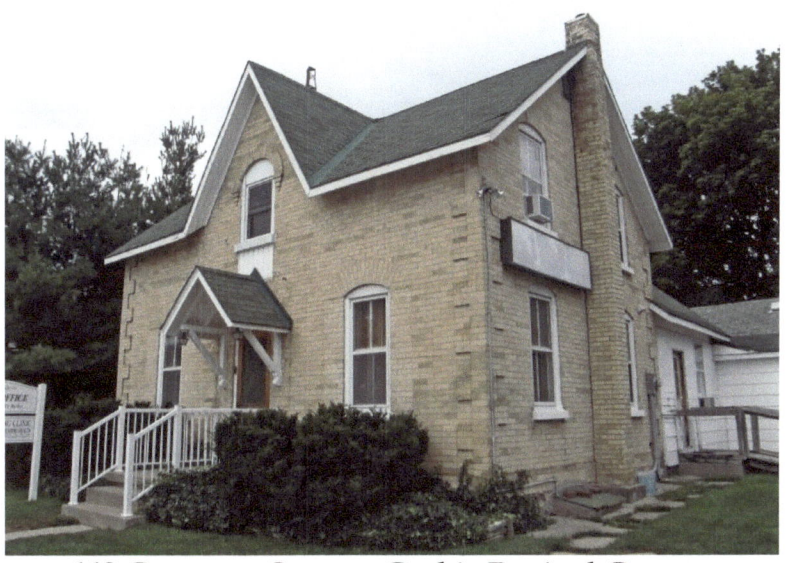

669 Gustavus Street – Gothic Revival Cottage
– arched voussoir over attic window, corner quoins

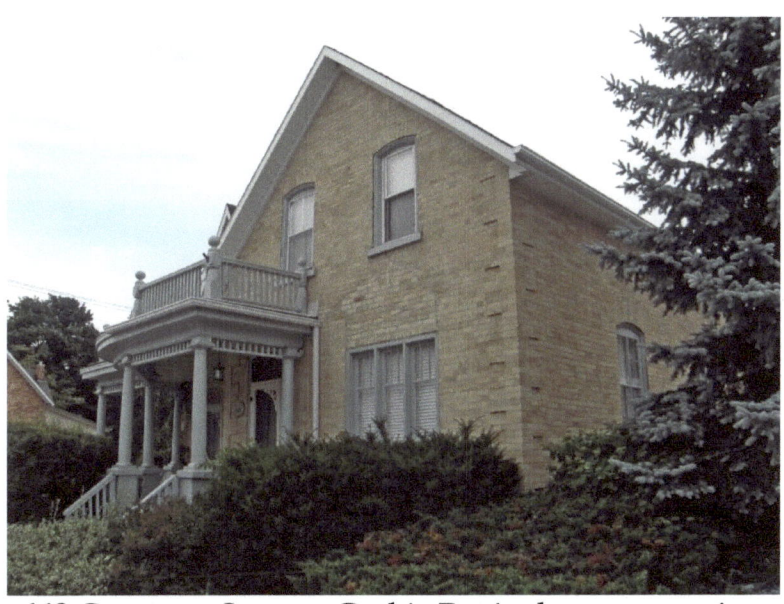

668 Gustavus Street – Gothic Revival, corner quoins,
2nd floor balcony

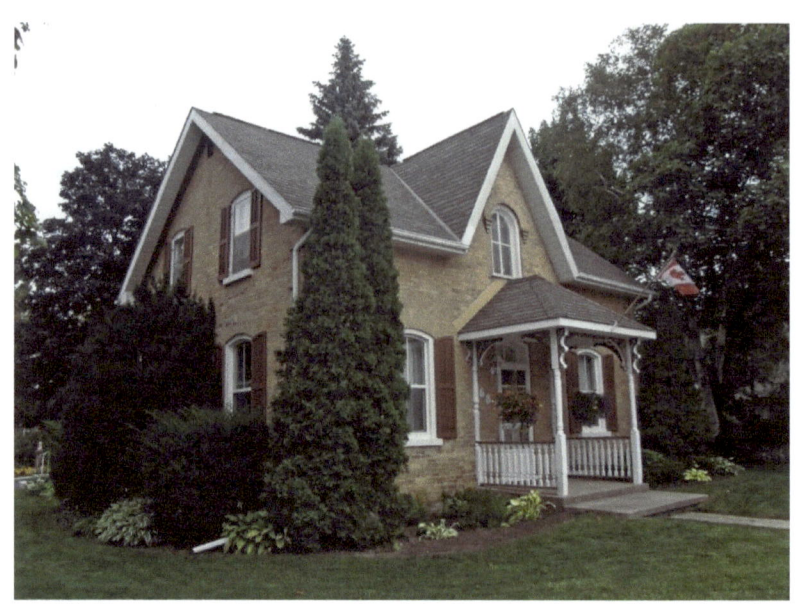

687 Gustavus Street – Gothic Revival – yellow brick

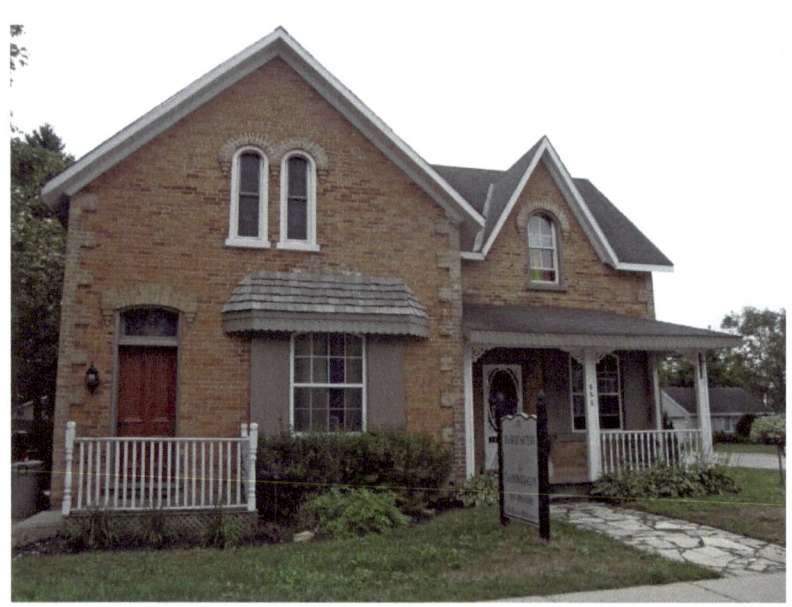

686 Gustavus Street – Gothic Revival, arched vousoirs over upper windows, corner quoining – red brick

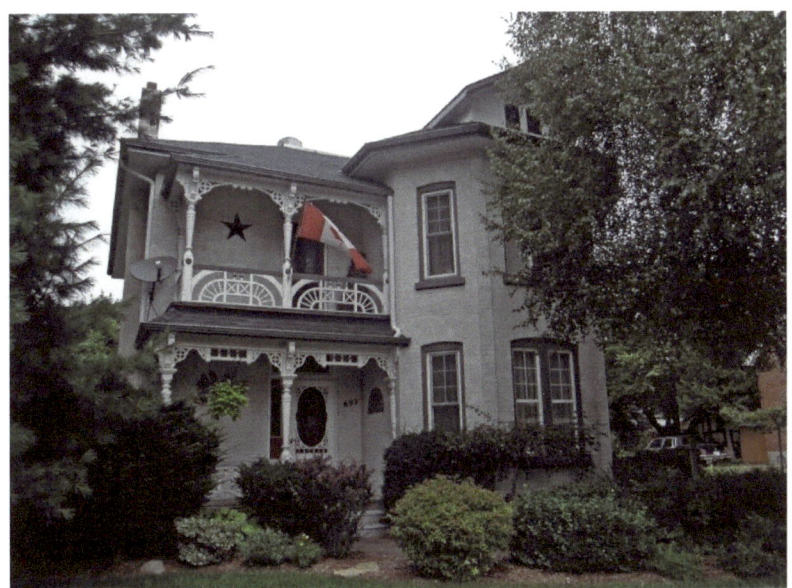

697 Gustavus Street – Italianate style – elaborate decorative
fretwork on the balcony and porch, two-storey tower-like bay

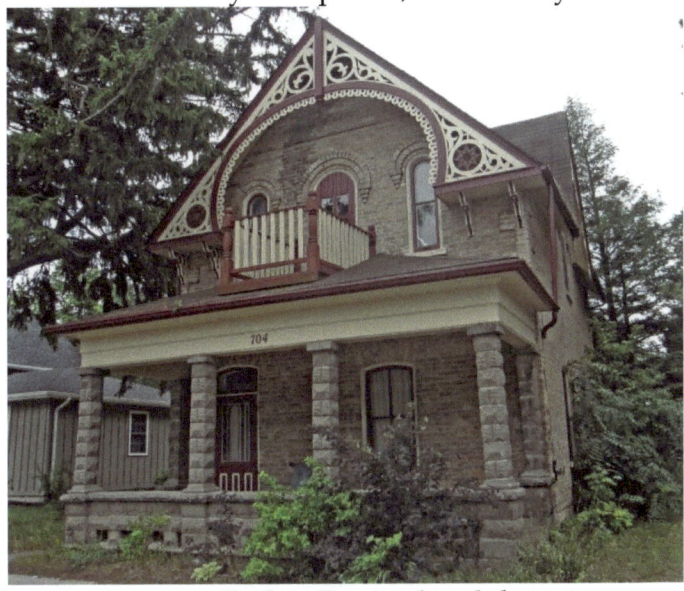

704 Gustavus Street – Gothic Revival – elaborate verge boards,
Romanesque style arched window voussoirs – yellow brick

Chatsworth

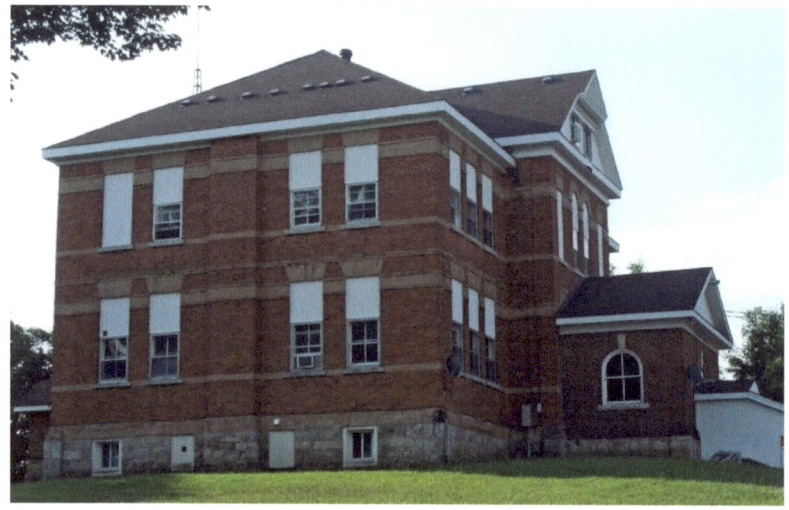

Banding

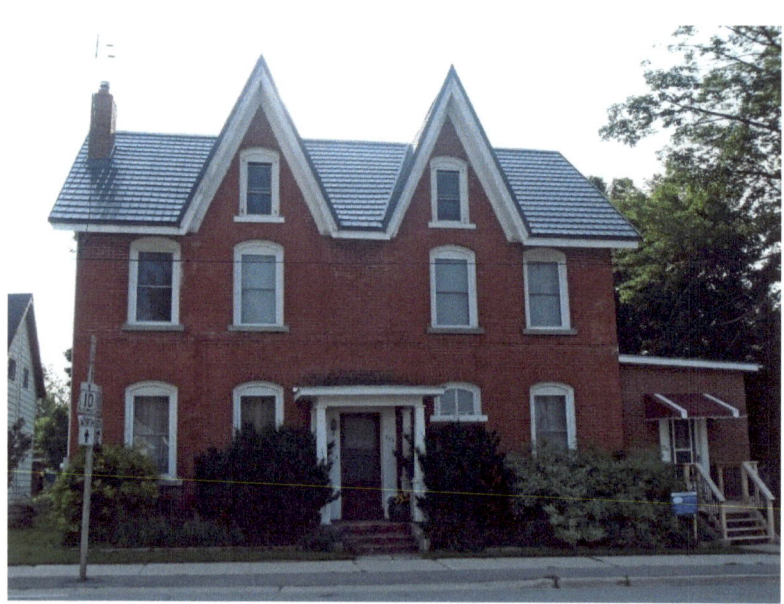

Gothic Revival

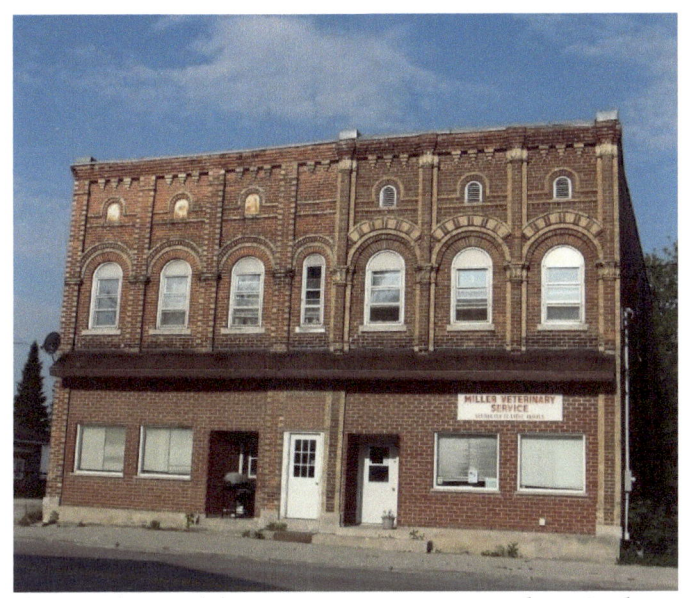

Bevelled dentil moulding, Romanesque style window arches, dichromatic brickwork, pilasters

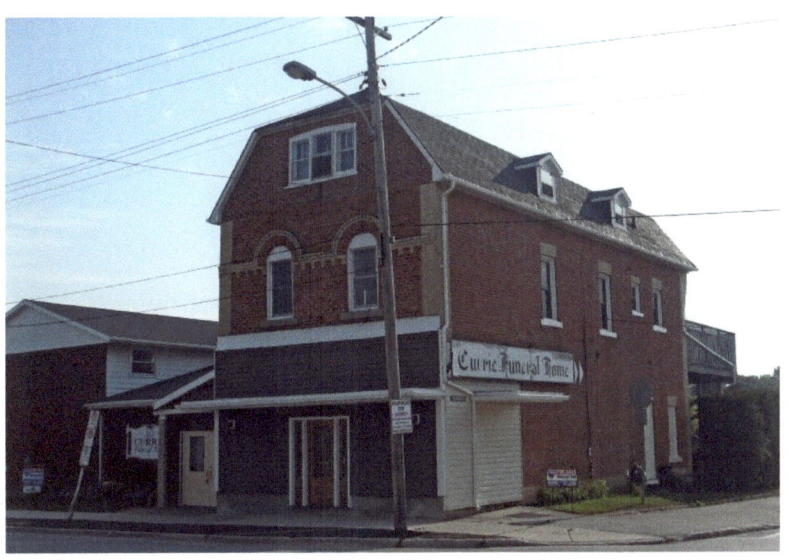

Dichromatic brickwork, dormers in attic

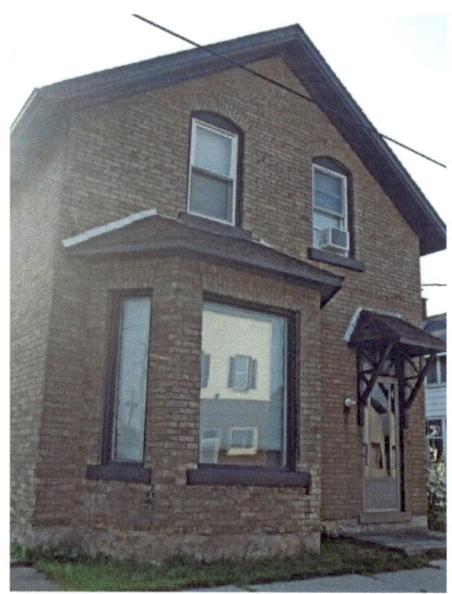

Gothic Revival, bay window

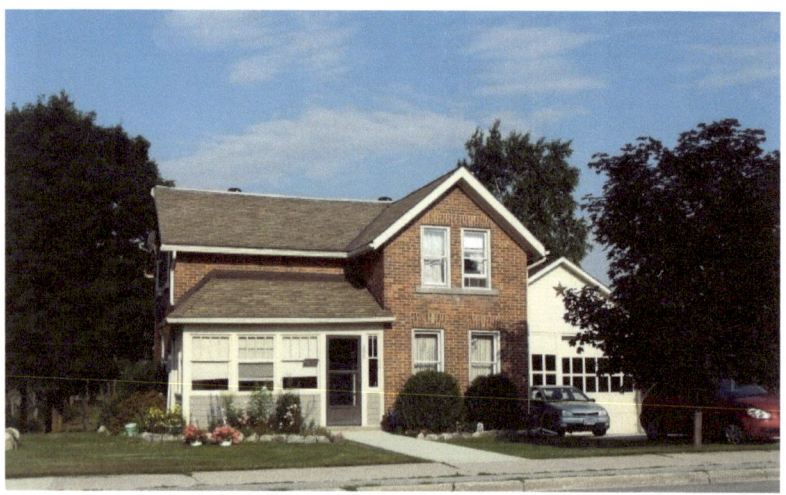

Gothic

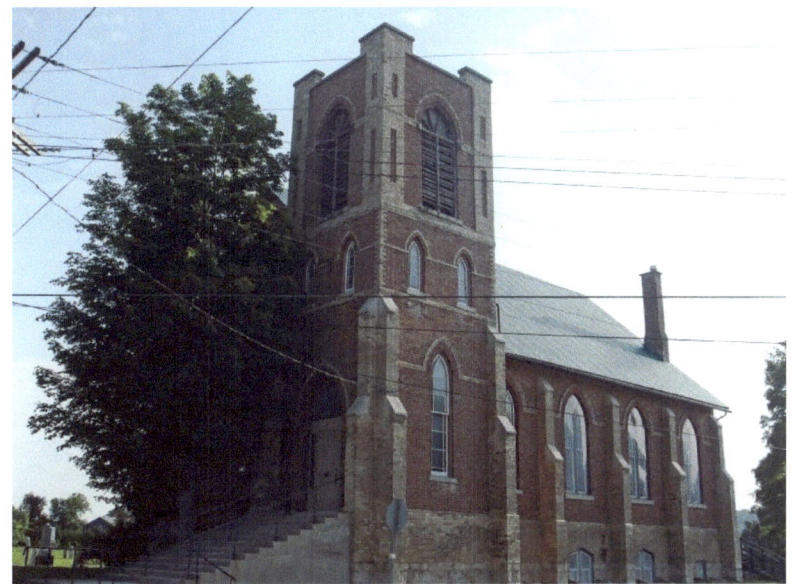

Chatsworth United Church – buttresses, lancet windows, banding, dichromatic brickwork

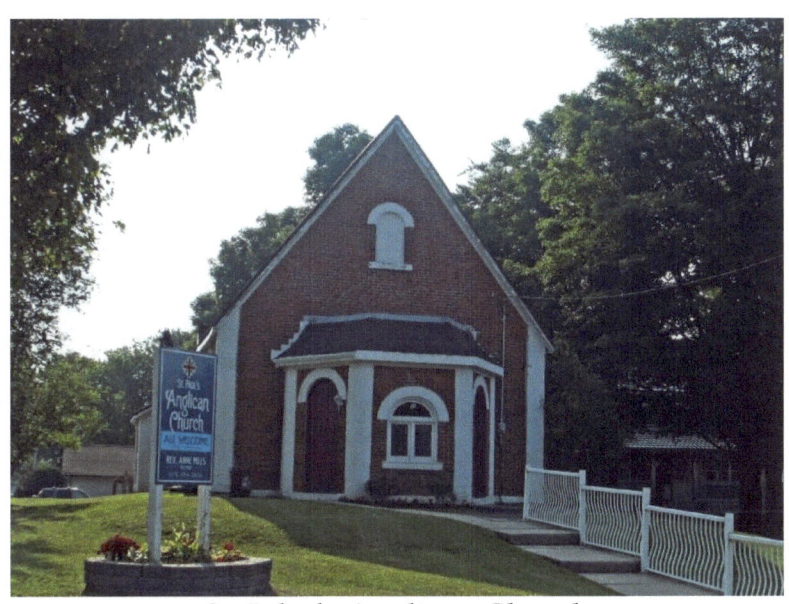

St. John's Anglican Church

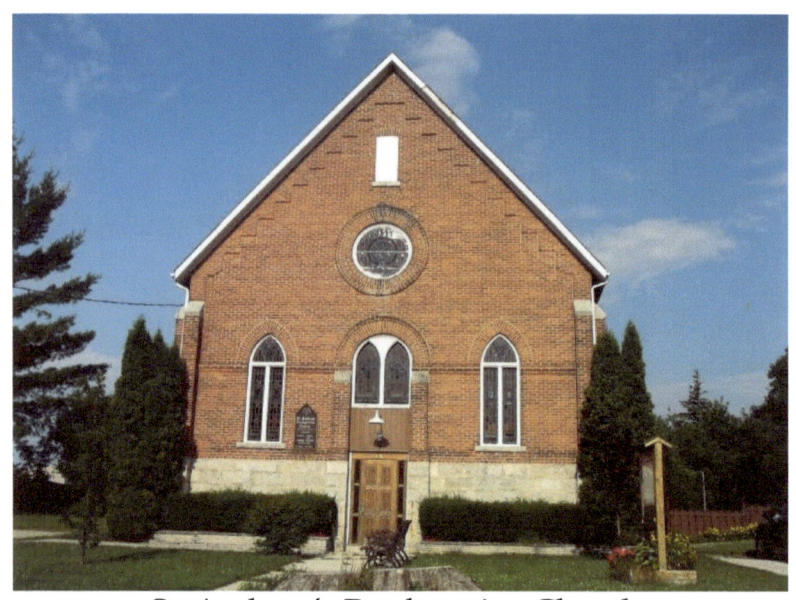

St. Andrew's Presbyterian Church,
Romanesque style door voussoir

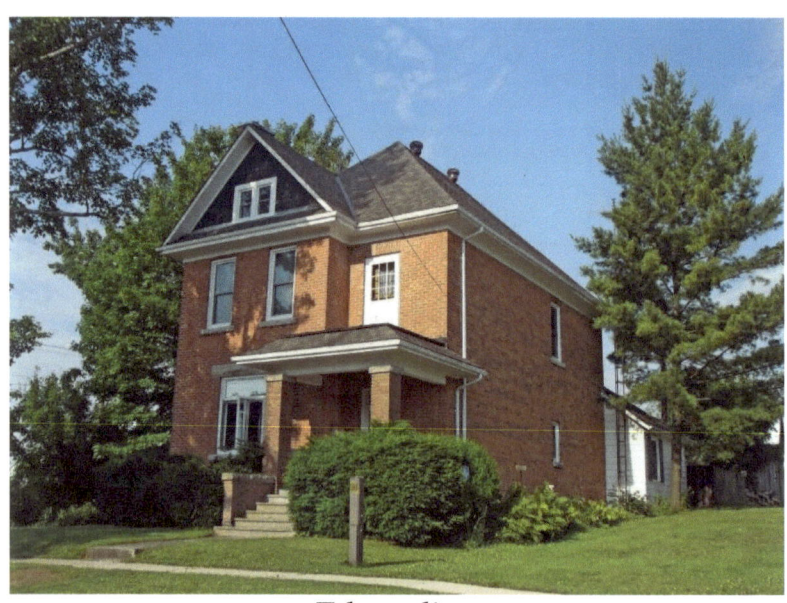

Edwardian

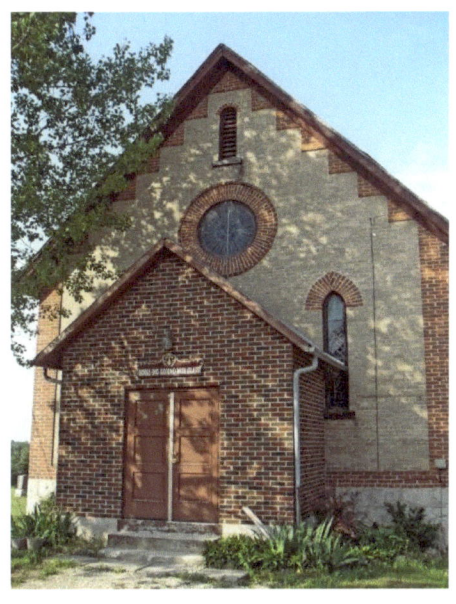

Dichromatic brickwork

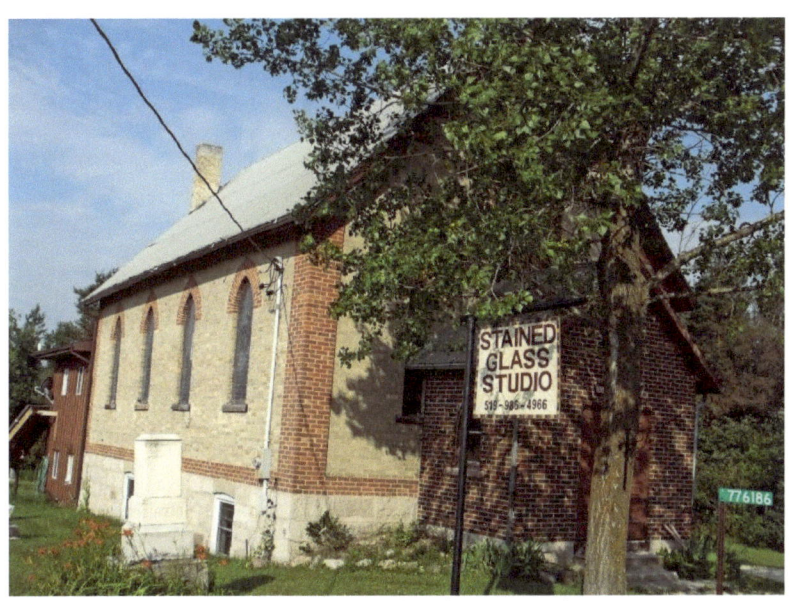

Now a Stained Glass Studio

Dornoch

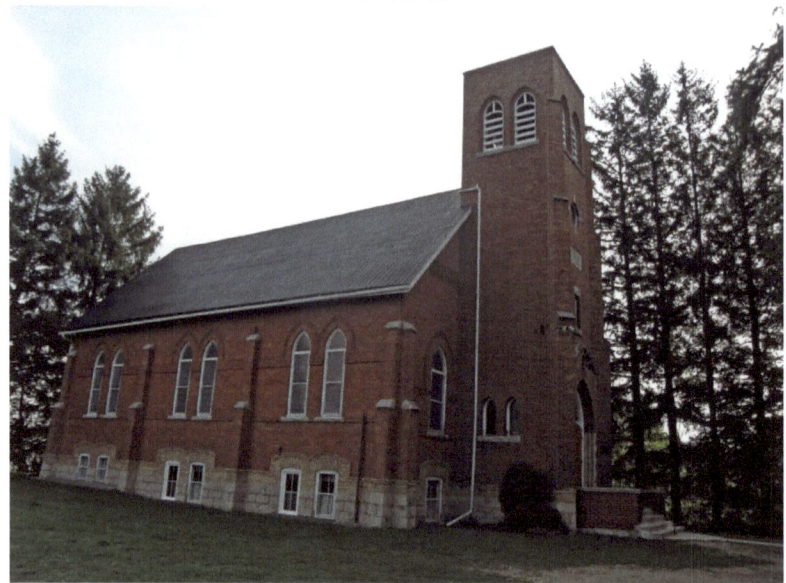

Latona Presbyterian Church built 1920
Buttresses, lancet windows

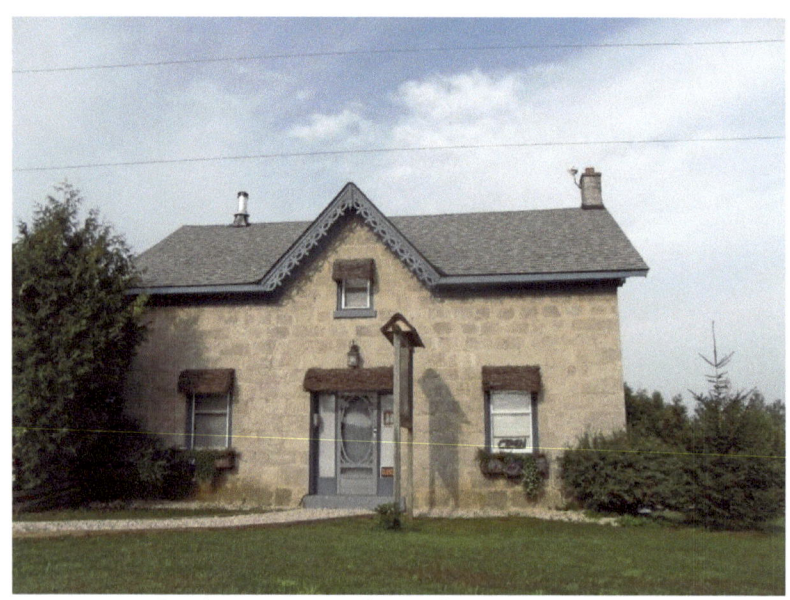

Gothic – verge board trim on gable

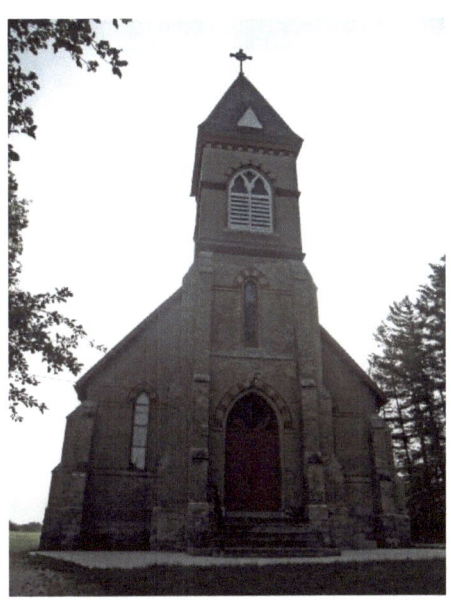

St. Paul's Catholic Church, Dornoch

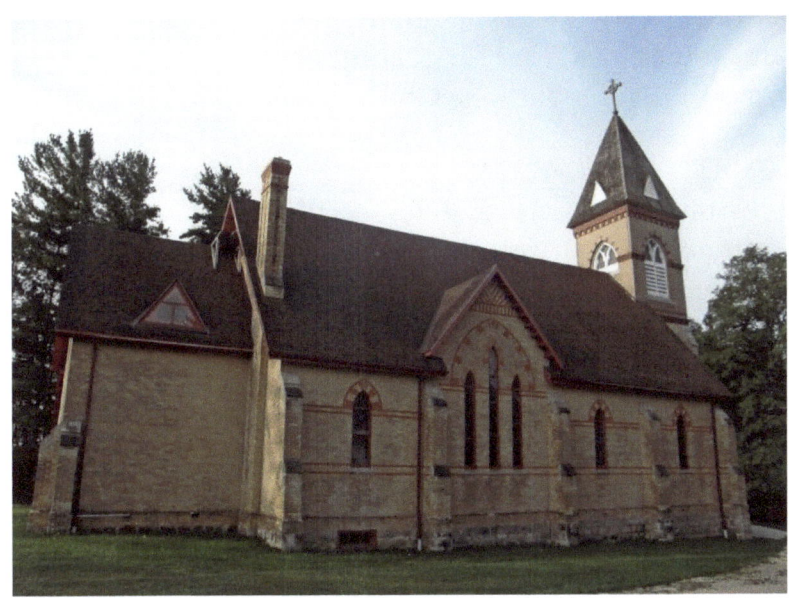

Banding, dichromatic brickwork, buttresses, lancet windows

Architectural Terms

Banding: Different materials, colours or textures used in horizontal bands along a wall. Example: St. Paul's Catholic Church, Dornoch, Page 45	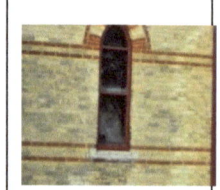
Brackets: a decorative or weight-bearing structural element which forms a right angle with one side against a wall and the other under a projecting surface such as an eave or roof. Example: 824 Goderich Street, see Page 13	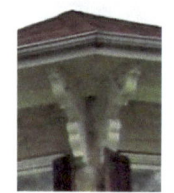
Buttress: a masonry structure built against or projecting from a wall which serves to support or reinforce the wall. In Canadian architecture, they are sometimes used for decoration. Example: St. Paul's Catholic Church, Dornoch, Page 45	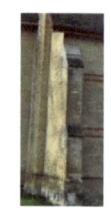
Cobblestone architecture: Refers to the use of cobblestones embedded in mortar as a method for erecting walls on houses and commercial buildings. Example: Port Elgin High School, see Page 27	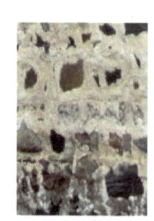
Cornice Return: decorative element on the end of a gable. Example: Mill Street, Port Elgin, See Page 30	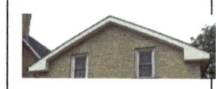

Dentil Moulding: an even series of rectangles used as ornamental decoration in cornices. Example: Port Elgin High School, see Page 28	
Dichromatic brickwork: the use of two colours of brick, tile or slate to decorate a façade. Example: St. Paul's Catholic Church, Dornoch, Page 45	
Dormer: (French for "sleep") a gable end window that pierces through the plane of a sloping roof surface to create usable space in the top floor or attic of a building by adding headroom. Example: 850 Goderich Street, see Page 14	
Finial: ornament added to the top of a gable, pinnacle, canopy or spire – a Gothic element. Example: Port Elgin High School, see Page 27	
Fretwork: interlaced decorative design resembling a bracket. Example: see Page 8	
Gable: the triangular portion of a wall between the edges of a sloping roof. Example: see Page 8	

Hipped Roof: a roof where all sides slope downwards to the walls with no gables. Example: 819 George Street, Port Elgin, Page 14	
Keystones and Voussoirs: a voussoir is a wedge-shaped element used in building an arch. A keystone is the central stone that locks all the stones into position, allowing the arch to bear weight. A keystone is often enlarged and embellished. Example: see Page 6	
Lancet Window: a tall, narrow window with a pointed arch at its top. Example: Latona Presbyterian Church, see Page 44	
Quoin: masonry blocks at the corner of a wall, often a decorative feature, usually larger or of a different colour than the rest of the wall. Example: 656 Market Street, Port Elgin, see Page 19	
Verge boards: also called bargeboards – hang from the projecting end of a roof and are often elaborately carved and ornamented. Example: 704 Gustavus Street, Port Elgin, Page 37	

Port Elgin's Building Styles

Edwardian, 1900-1930 – This style bridges the ornate and elaborate styles of the Victorian era and the simplified styles of the 20th century. Balanced facades, simple roof lines, dormer windows, large front porches, and smooth brick surfaces are its characteristics. Example: see Page 23	
Georgian, before 1860 – This style began with the British King Georges in the 18th century. These buildings have balanced facades around a central door, medium-pitched gable roofs, and small paned windows. Example: 650 Market Street, Page 18	
Gothic Revival, 1830-1890 – These decorative buildings have sharply-pitched gables with highly detailed vergeboards, pointed-arch window openings, and dichromatic brickwork. It is a common style in Ontario. Example: 686 Gustavus Street, Page 36	
Italianate, 1850-1900 – It has wide-bracketed eaves, belvederes, wrap-around verandahs. Example: 824 Goderich Street, Page 13	

www.ingramcontent.com/pod-product-compliance
Lightning Source LLC
Chambersburg PA
CBHW040923180526
45159CB00002BA/586